$12 —

W9-CLQ-934

Wolverine farm publishing's

MATTER JOURNAL

VOLUME **12** PRESS

FORT COLLINS, COLORADO

For information please address:
Wolverine Farm Publishing, PO BOX 814,
Fort Collins, CO 80522.

FIRST EDITION
11 10 9 8 7 6 5 4 3 2 1

Printed in Boulder, CO on recycled paper according to industry standards established by the Green Press Initiative. Overall, we try to keep this magazine as honest as possible. We are small and want to remain that way. You may be as big as you like.

ISBN: 978-0-9823372-2-6
ISSN: 1548-1841
LCCN: 2004-214172

Ahead, Beyond

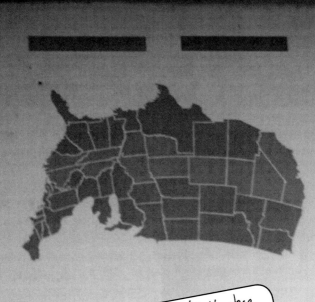

Nothing in the world can take the place of persistence. Talent will not; nothing is more common than unsuccessful men with talent. Genius will not; unrewarded genius is almost a proverb. Education will not; the world is full of educated derelicts. Persistence and determination are omnipotent. The slogan "PRESS ON" has solved and will always solve the problems of the human race.

~Attributed to Calvin Coolidge

TABLE OF CONTENTS

HERE & THERE IN THIS ISSUE

PHOTO & ART CREDITS

EVERYWHERE ELSE

Julie Larson...120,124-129
Charles Malone....................................2, 3, 10, 38, 39, 106, 107
David Mitchell...24, 26, 62, 63, 144, 145
Will Oldham...84, 89
Leslie Patterson (photographs)..96
Susan Hazel Rich (hand-lettered titles)..................................96, 136
Sue Ring deRosset..70, 73, 77, 80, 135

MATTER is
Jason Hardung : Utility Editor
Megan Schiel : Managing Editor
Charles Malone : Poetry Editor
Todd Simmons : Designer/Publisher

Special thanks to: Bethany Kopp, Laurie Hanselmann, Andrew Bohn, Evan P Schneider, Sue Ring deRosset, John Major Jenkins and his print shop, Anne Macdonald, Bryan Simpson, Gary Wockner, Erin Hughes, The Bean Cyclers, and all the Matter Bookstore Volunteers who make this effort possible and worthwhile.

The relevance of this issue only became more apparent the longer we delayed publication. In our frenzied effort to pull this issue shut our fair town lost one weekly newspaper (granted, the hollowed-out *Fort Collins Now*) and the main daily, *The Coloradoan*, sent production sixty miles south to Denver. Some of the photos in this issue were taken the day after The *Coloradoan* shut down their press, when the two remaining workmen were extracting the last of the ink from the enormous machines. In some ways, we dedicate this issue to those two men, who had ink running all the way up their arms, and some smeared on their faces.

Pressing On
A Dispatch from the Frontlines and the Headlines

Non-Fiction by Joshua Zaffos

"I am an exile from newspapers because of the most grievous sin of all—I have lost my belief. I no longer believe that the front page, the business page, the sports page, the arts page can tell a story that matters."
— *Charles Bowden*, Blood Orchid

"Remember what I told you a long time ago?" my grandmother asked me over the phone. My ears perked, thinking she was on the verge of revealing some sage advice that she earned through her long years. "There's no future in the papers."

Grandma Sue's hint of ancient wisdom was actually a warning, a taunt of sorts, that she likes to repeat to me quite regularly when I see her in person back East or occasionally when we talk over the phone: Newspapers are a dead end for a smart fellow like her youngest grandson.

My grandmother wasn't disclosing some lesson gained from a career as an editor at the *Washington Post* or a beat reporter for *Newsweek*. I presume her shared insight was something she picked up watching Fox News.

"They're giving it away for free here," Grandma told me, "here" being New York City and "it" being the city's tabloid dailies, including Rupert Murdoch's *New York Post*. "And there's nothing in there. It's all crap. People, they've got the intercom now."

I love my grandma, even if she sometimes confuses an in-house communication system with the World Wide Web. And I don't argue with her over the phone. What's the point? I'm glad I still have regular conversations with her, and, besides, her diagnosis of the press is only partly skewed. The *New York Post* is filled with crap, and publishers are facing a crisis. That's why dailies are dumping free copies on potential readers, and, more critically, slashing bureaus, beats and staff and even closing their doors.

It's happening up and down the print-media food chain, and I am a minor witness to the carnage. My own (mis) adventures working for local, independent newspapers—far cries from the *Post* and most other New York City media—have both ended with abrupt closures and tears in beers.

How rough has grown the jungle of print media?

It's nearly impossible to post an accurate account of the industry's well being, if only because the casualties keep rolling in. Writing on the topic requires constant dismal revisions. Not that the prognosis has really changed from my grandmother's conclusion. After weighing the consequences of job cuts and profit-based management at our country's newspapers, media critics determined 2008 to be a disastrous landmark for the press: Worst. Year. Ever.

In February, the *New York Times* cut 100 jobs, the paper's first staff layoff ever. Later in the year, the newspaper revealed that its stock value had plummeted 15 percent in a single month. To stave off a more severe disaster in December, the company borrowed $225 million against the value of its Manhattan headquarters to augment its dwindling cash flow.

The *Los Angeles Times* cut 150 newsroom jobs (17 percent of the department) and 100 additional staff; the *Chicago Tribune* lopped off 80 positions. Both major dailies are part of the Tribune Company, which has made similarly deep cuts to daily newspapers in Baltimore, Orlando, and elsewhere. The corporation declared bankruptcy in December, citing $13 billion in debts.

In June, McClatchy Co., the third-largest newspaper publisher in the US, disclosed it would eliminate 1,400 jobs, roughly 10 percent of its workforce, among its 30 dailies across the country. For those who survived the purge, there is a locked-in yearlong pay freeze.

E.W. Scripps, which owns newspapers in 15 states, including the *Rocky Mountain News*, announced in the summer that the value of its print holdings had dropped by $874 million. Before the end of the year, Scripps put the *Rocky* up for sale, claiming it would likely close down the 150-year-old newspaper if a buyer didn't emerge in early 2009.

Gannett, the country's largest print publisher, declared a loss of $2.4 billion in the value of its 84 daily and nearly 900 non-daily newspapers, including the *USA Today*. A first round of August layoffs chopped 1,000 jobs, which was followed by another cut of 3,000 positions in October, totaling more than 10 percent of the company's staff. Perversely, but not surprisingly, Gannett's summer staff reduction caused its stock to jump on Wall Street.

We are watching the equivalent of media climate change, to use everyone's favorite disaster parlance of late, and this is the tip of the iceberg that has started to melt away in the twenty-first century. Unfortunately, due to consolidation of media ownership and other financial forces, companies are getting rewarded for dedicating fewer and fewer resources to journalism and writing.

Where are the media corporations investing their dollars? In September, Gannett spent $135 million to purchase a controlling stake in CareerBuilder, the online job board, which is co-owned by Tribune and McClatchy. And while media corporations are facing plummeting stock earnings and disappearing advertising revenue, the bosses aren't exactly starving. For the third quarter of 2008, Gannett actually exceeded analysts' revenue projections and earned $158 million in net income. The company's CEO Craig Dubow, who pledged to take a 17 percent pay cut in "a show of solidarity" with his newspapers' rank-and-file, made about $7.5 million in 2008, including salary, stock options, and a bonus.

It obviously costs millions to run these corporations, and the largest media empires have the most to lose in this topsy-turvy moment. Regardless of where we live, shrinking resources at institutional newspapers, like the *New York Times* and *Chicago Tribune*, are a major loss to our national community as a whole. But independent and alternative papers must also tread the rising waters and sinking ad revenue, although they're much more likely to drown.

Smaller daily and community weekly papers are cutting staff, closing bureaus abroad and in state capitals. Independent papers, like alternative newsweeklies, which distribute for free and rely entirely on ad dollars, are faced with corporate buyouts or shutting down. The pressures have led to somewhat troubling trends among altweeklies, which pride themselves on their independence.

Village Voice Media now owns 15 alternative newsweeklies, in New York, Los Angeles, Houston, Denver, and several other major cities. Creative Loafing runs six altweeklies, including ones in Chicago, Washington, D.C., and Atlanta. Both companies have instituted staff cuts at several papers, and other independently owned altweeklies have expressed reservations over the direction of these decidedly corporate ventures.

When I first accepted a job as a staff writer at the *Rocky Mountain Bullhorn*, an alternative newsweekly in Fort Collins, Colorado, in late 2004, a mentoring friend let out a devilish hoot upon hearing my decision. "Have you ever worked at a weekly?" she asked. I had not, and she explained to me that writing at a weekly publication somehow combines the manic rush of filing stories at a daily newspaper with the more exhaustive demands that come with a monthly magazine, where articles are expected to develop from

extensive reporting and offer much more than the five W's.

A weekly doesn't have someone on a deadline everyday, yet something is always due. The production doesn't give many breaths or breaks, and the pace is constantly frenetic, which induces a sort of crash-and-burn atmosphere.

"And you and everyone you work with will always be going crazy," my friend told me.

She was right.

Almost everybody at an independent weekly newspaper is overworked and underpaid, and at the darkest hours we feel alone in that capacity. That's not true, at a newspaper or in the surrounding universe; there are many more and equally as taxing jobs in the world. But when you are spending 60-plus hours a week working at, and then sometimes sleeping under a desk, it's way too easy to find moments to feel both sorry about yourself and for yourself.

The staff is typically a small band of creative-neurotic types. I've seen coworkers starve themselves, drop shots of whiskey for breakfast, suffer panic attacks requiring EMT attention, and, literally, chew off their fingers. In the middle of an intense story or a chaotic week, I would sometimes wake up with a compulsion to violently dry heave before getting into the day. Working at a small altweekly makes smoking cigarettes seem like a healthy lifestyle choice (I do not wish to count the number of former coworkers who started or resumed smoking while employed at a paper).

At a small weekly newspaper, everybody is always going crazy.

Sound like hell? It's actually great. There is a euphoria that sometimes rises like a vapor from this mayhem, a byproduct of collaborating on something creative and essential.

That might sound a little arrogant, but this intense feeling, channeling the heaves and highs, is what good writing—good storytelling—is for me. And, to be direct, most writers are at least a little arrogant.

The intense feeling is what I think of when someone asks if I am a member of the press (I haven't seen a newspaper printing press since I went on a second-grade field trip). To me, the *press* is the sleeplessness and self-immolation, the euphoria and drunkenness that come with telling stories with a balance of detail and urgency. The *press* is that unbearable feeling that what we are doing has meaning to our society, whether as information, influence, or entertainment.

It is a great and humbling responsibility reporting and writing for a community, and it is something I am grateful to be paid to do. I love the crush of an idea or a person that I have discovered or been introduced to, and the snap in my brain that *this* would be an amazing or beautiful or entertaining story. Then comes the compulsion that people should read (or hear or see) about this and feel the spark that I do.

This is the press that is in trouble, more so than print media as an industry. It's the thing that feeds and connects writers, producers, and broadcasters of news in all its forms. We report and write because we want to make a difference. We want to deliver meaning.

These days, as print media cannibalizes itself, we are losing that urgency to make sure what we report and write is meaningful. Some writers recognize it as morale loss or viral fear. Middle managers spin it as doing More With

Less. Readers of daily newspapers get shallow stories with glancing insight from publications that are purposely streamlined. Reporters rarely get to develop relationships with sources and communities. When people complain to me about the Gannett-owned daily newspaper in our city, they often say that the paper fails to connect the dots.

This is supposed to be the great advantage to working at an independent publication, particularly an altweekly: the freedom to dig deeper and write stories that matter. It's partly what led me to abandon a modest freelance writing lifestyle for a job that made me wake up nauseous. The trick, I learned, is staying in business.

The Worst Year Ever for newspapers certainly proved challenging to my journalistic career. In May 2008, I was a part of an independent altweekly, the *Rocky Mountain Chronicle*, which shut down a few months ahead of the curve in terms of the year's media trauma. It was an experience I was repeating for the second time in just twenty-seven months.

After twelve roller-coaster months at the *Bullhorn*, the five-year-old weekly newspaper suddenly went out of business in early 2006, while we were finishing an issue that would never go to print.

I was heartbroken, along with everyone I worked with, but there was also a strange sense of relief. Amid the chaos that we constantly worked in, it was hard to ignore the financial pressures that the organization was facing. That we were shutting down wasn't a total surprise, but the timing was a shock.

The same heartbreak strikes when bureaus, beats, and jobs

are cut at daily newspapers, when TV stations consolidate their newsrooms. On journalism list-serves that I read, prize-winning reporters have shared their decisions to accept voluntary layoffs, rather than continuing to work under the shadow of job losses, redundancy orders, merged beats, and pay freezes.

Just seven months after the *Bullhorn* closed, a good friend announced that she wanted to launch the *Chronicle* as a new altweekly newspaper in Fort Collins. Born and raised in the city, she recognized the value of an independent newspaper pursuing narrative stories about the people and culture of our region. Our readership grew steadily, but even more impressive to me, as the news editor, were the number of sources and untold stories that emerged.

The *Chronicle* started in October 2006. We engaged in investigative and in-depth stories, critical music and arts writing, and general quirk. Among editors, we had a lot of passionate debates over the significance and mission of our publication and writing, and the meaning of words like "investigative," "alternative," and "edgy." Those discussions may have bordered on the pretentious and the precise, but we were genuine in our desire to write meaningful stories.

When our publisher consulted with other altweekly bosses, they told her she was crazy. Flush some money down a toilet instead, they said. Since altweeklies rely almost exclusively on ad revenue for income, the sub-industry has taken a particularly harsh hit due to free online advertising through venues like Craigslist and the overall sagging economy, which has left local businesses with fewer dollars to spend on advertising.

The experienced altweekly publishers were apparently right

about the high odds of getting a startup paper up and running; something we really already knew from the last experience. After a not particularly lengthy existence of just 20 months, the *Chronicle* announced it would cease printing amid daunting prospects for financial viability.

If you've never worked at a small business that shuts down because it cannot sustain itself, I can tell you this: It catches you like a bad breakup to a good relationship and leaves a lot of unanswered questions. At first, a measure of sadness is cushioned in a daze. Grief quickly gives way to anger. At a homegrown newspaper, there is this feeling: Our work is not yet done. There are stories still to be told.

The week after we learned of the closure, I received a handwritten letter from a woman with claims of police brutality and political corruption, begging our paper to look into her leads. She may have been a crackpot—sorting through print-worthy sources and stories is one way to dive into the *press*—but she had chosen to write our paper, and not others in the city, for a reason. I left the letter pinned to a corkboard after I had cleaned out my office.

We are living through the somewhat predictable circumstances of corporate control and consolidated ownership of media. The current bleak state of journalism has been a slow train coming. The recession is a stretch of poorly maintained rails and the Internet is a behemoth beast standing on the tracks.

Grandma Sue isn't totally off base in her assessment about the Internet replacing print media. More people now get their news online than by reading a paper. The *New York Times* estimates that it has ten Web readers for every one who turns through the print edition. The Web has competed, more than complemented, print publications.

From an operational point of view, the catch is that people expect to read for free on the Internet, and businesses expect to pay less to advertise online. From an informational angle, the trend is leading to shorter and more glancing articles and coverage, even if it opens opportunities for multimedia work. We have taken the act of reading and begun transforming it into another way of staring at an electronic screen.

There are some inspiring digital manifestations (among a range of examples, there is the Center for Investigative Reporting and MediaStorm). But corporate-chain media barons are also trying to conquer a new medium and return to the salad days of ludicrous profits and booming stocks. For example, Gannett has kicked up the visibility of its online reporting and resources, as part of its corporate restructuring. The company now calls reporters "mojos," or mobile journalists. The transition smacks of re-branding, a marketing strategy to perhaps show that Gannett's newspapers are hip with blogging and the Web, rather than a meaningful new model of journalism.

I do not blame Gannett or Craigslist for the failure of the independent papers where I worked. I do not blame the competition from other local newspapers or blogs for our end. But I lament that we have created an environment (and, yes, We The People are responsible for the current media landscape) that is so prohibitive to running a newspaper that delivers stories that matter, where the *press* flows for writers and readers—and publishers, too.

We are losing the venues we have developed to tell stories. And we are giving a jaded set of choices to writers and readers. So, now we must learn how to tell stories all over

17

again. We must learn how to tell stories on a computer screen. We have to keep learning how to tell stories on TV, so most of those resources don't go into entrapping sexual predators at anonymous houses. And we must learn how to keep telling stories on paper.

The pangs of the *press* kept a few *Chronicle* staff members searching for life after print. We had told readers we would explore options. We looked at online formats and spoke with people behind nonprofit journalism ventures, where funding comes from charitable foundations and community members—kind of like public radio and television.

The *Chronicle* did find signs of support and encouragement for continuing as an online publication, possibly with a monthly print issue. But we also recognized that we would be constantly scrambling for operating funds. The nonprofit model was a way to get around the void of advertising dollars as revenue, but grant funding is a tricky avenue to travel during a slow economy.

To be honest and with apologies to our community, I think we were burnt out. I was burnt out. The task felt monumental and, after three months of meetings, I felt pretty emotionless when our remaining crew decided we would give up our revival attempt. When it came time to pen an announcement about the decision to officially end our efforts, I made it as brief as possible. The 100-word missive was more memo than eulogy.

People still approach me—including souls I have never met before—and ask what's up with the *Chronicle*, when will it restart, or when a new publication might arrive in its place. A friend of mine can't accept that we have exhausted all of our options. A woman at the bar refuses to accept my answers about the closure. A barista from one of the downtown coffee shops listens to my explanations and then says, with a pout, "Well, you left us with nothing to read."

When my grandmother or anyone else tells me newspapers and the narrative forms of writing that we associate with print media are dead, I think of the book-versus-film debate. So many more people see the film but never read the book. The film makes more money than the book; it's more successful in those terms. But people who read the book *and* see the movie almost always say the book is better. Perhaps for the effort and time it requires; perhaps because of what reading asks of our imagination.

There is a future in the papers, but it's not going to look like the past. Hopefully, it won't resemble the present too much either. My guess is that most daily newspapers will become online enterprises. The loss of the morning paper on our front step might be the cost of allowing stock values to steer the media industry.

As for the outlook of independent and meaningful journalism, it will be in the ventures that tap into the Web and all that it has to offer while also pursuing more traditional forms of reporting and storytelling. If that sounds vague, it's because it's meant to: If I had a proper bead on the future, I suspect I would still have a job at an independent newspaper in Northern Colorado.

In July 2008, a subscriber to the *Raleigh News & Observer* took action in a most American way. He announced plans to sue the daily paper for cutting the size of its news section and firing 70 staff members. The reader claimed the newspaper had broken its contract with subscribed readers.

The lawsuit borders on frivolous, but it's a reminder that newspapers and the media—regardless of or, at least, in addition to their responsibility to stockholders—have a pulsing obligation to the communities they serve. To tell stories that matter and stoke the *press*.

TELL STORIES THAT MATTER.

WWW.MATTERDAILY.ORG

COMING SOON VIA WEB &
PRINT SUPPLEMENTS

Christopher Caruso

Man Hit By Car

The Event

There were after effects –

time doesn't stop
but perception becomes
a warped record

so it skips ahead
backwards   –you get
a photo album
of dislocated memories.

The Scenery

> * Sidewalk shrubs keep a distance
> * A split open shopping bag's synthesis with a tree
> * A store window yells "Going Out Of Business"
> * Soda cans and beer bottles left to gather dust
> * A crystal spider-web newly formed

The Follow Up

There is only so much that makes the news. War, lack

of health, and prices of gasoline. A phone call received
to verify an experience: only questions no answers.

The Next Day

Somewhere there is a poem
and a thought (concern).
But there are distractions:
bills, taxes inevitable things.

M. K. Leonard

The Unified Field

In gray overalls he
works the space of garden soil by shovel turns.
June light, warming arms and earth,
fuels his muscles for the task and
releases the scent of long-ago pine.
Shffh, lift, turn. Shffh, lift, turn.
Mounds of earth line up like tiny mountains
whose valleys will drink the next rain.
Shffh, lift, turn for an hour.
Task done, he rests outstretched on
nearby grass, in the feathered shade
of a locust tree. Head cupped in hand,
he waits for the soil to reveal its needs.
Two robins decide;
they alight and peck for worms and bugs.
Poke, pick, swallow.
In silent welcome he watches the birds
who enjoy the feast the earth yields,
who acknowledge him with easy nods
as they might a benefactor, protector, or friend.
He is all three
in the hushed, radiant
universe of this holy moment,
this steward who tends the earth
and watches the birds who
labor near him in the soil,
all aligned in this great conjunction.

Bella Jordanian

Non-Fiction by Kurt Caswell

So then, you'll never guess what happened. We had just come to a sort-of stopping place in our conversation about relationships and marriage, and so naturally, after the food and the beers at Scotland's version of the Olive Garden—Bella Italia—Scott, my old pal from high school and the best man at my wedding, which, by the way, resulted in a divorce five years later (which was about three years ago), got up and headed north to the facilities. He'd just confessed the hardships and struggles he and his wife, Kacey, had passed through, empathized with my plight, and acknowledged that it could have easily been him. (And her, of course.) But you know, they had the children, and maybe that helped bind them together in a way childless couples are not bound together, and they had the house on some beautiful acreage in southern Oregon, and yes, they also loved each other, and so they worked through the garbage to come out on the other side.

"Now things are better than ever," Scott said. And then, "You're not going to have children are you?"

"I'm gonna have a vasectomy," I said.

"Really? Well, it's not too awful bad," Scott said, rubbing his balding head. "You can't drive home on your own, but a long weekend will see you through recovery. Except you have to wait awhile afterwards before you can use it." Then he left for the loo.

That's when Tia came to my rescue, the hostess at the restaurant, and she arrested my descent into a minor depression, the kind that usually follows such a grave conversation especially after your buddy gets up for a piss and you're left sitting alone in Inverness, Macbeth's happy town, fiddling with your fork or napkin or whatever.

"Where you from?" she asked.

She was the most gorgeous creature I'd seen all day.

NOTE: The last line in this piece was inspired by Dubravka Ugresic's short story "A Hot Dog in a Warm Bun," translated by Michael Henry Heim, and published in The Sex Box: Sex. San Francisco: Chronicle Books, 1996.

Shoulder length black hair, kinda ratty and witchy, huge dark eyes like Bambi blinking at that raging forest fire, a long graceful line down the length of her tight black trousers, and the most unexpectedly perfect chest. She spoke in a dark smoker's voice, which, unbeknownst to me until then, kinda turned me on.

"From?" I said, always at odds about how to answer that question. "I live in Texas, but I'm not a Texan, that's certain. I grew up in Oregon. But I wasn't born there." Slow down, I thought, that's enough.

"Oregon," she said. "That's a beautiful place, isn't it? And what are you doing here? Just traveling?"

"Yeah," I said. "Just a summer journey. I'm here with an old friend, and we're seeing the country, climbing some mountains."

Then, getting to the point, "How long are you here?" she asked.

She spoke with an accent, not heavy, but certainly not Scottish. When Scott and I walked in the door earlier, she said, "Buona Sera," which made me hope that she was Italian, because I'd never really recovered from that Italian romance I'd had when I was backpacking through Europe 15 years ago.

"We're here just for the night," I said. "We head for Edinburgh in the morning. Then down to the Lake District to climb a mountain."

"That's not very long," she said, recognizing the obvious.

We followed that exchange with some other small talk until I spotted Scott on his way back. "So," I said, "if you had one night in Inverness, where would you spend it?"

"In my bed," she said.

"What?" I said.

"In my bed," she said again.

But I still wasn't convinced I'd heard her correctly,

and so, a little startled, a little hopeful, a little creeped-out, I nodded my head and said, "Aahhh."

Scott arrived at the table then, and she scooted away back to work. As we were settling the bill, she returned again, and this time slipped me a scrap of paper with her name and mobile phone number. "Tia," I said.

"If you want, maybe we can have a drink later," she said, bobbing her head from side to side.

"Dude," Scott told me, as we downed a bottle of wine at the hostel where we were staying, "if you don't call that number tonight, you're fuckin' crazy. You have to."

"Inverness," I mused. "This is really a great town. The best place we've been yet!"

We laughed.

"But I'm not sure I heard what I heard," I said. "Com'on. Who says that?"

"Shut up," Scott said. "That's what she said all right. And she was hot, hot, like Africa hot."

"Yeah, but com'on. There's something else. I mean, who says that?"

"Obviously she does," Scott said. He filled the glasses. "She's probably a guy," he said, and we laughed even harder.

Then something a little human leaked in, and there was a quiet moment between us as we looked across the roof tops onto the city. Scott said, "Yeah, but you have to remember that this guy is a person too."

"What?"

"You know, if you get into a situation I mean, and you reach down there and find out she's a guy. I mean, she's a human being too. Or he is. And you have to treat her like a person not like some freak."

"She's not a guy," I said. "Plus, who says I'll be doing any reaching."

"Com'on," Scott said. "'In my bed?' You'll be doing

some reaching. Com'on. This bottle is empty. Let's go get a beer."

So out we went onto the town and, conveniently, we walked right by Bella Italia. And there she was standing out front smoking a cigarette.

This was a curious position to be in. Was I going to cross the street and make good on Tia's offer, this perfect stranger in a foreign town? Gorgeous though she was, I am not a whore. Indeed, I'm a respectable professional guy. I'm a teacher, for Christ's sake. I'm a divorced man who might have become a father. I'm good counsel when my friends come knocking. I'm domestic; I bake bread, brew beer, mend fences and socks, keep a tidy house, fix leaky faucets and pull the weeds where they come up. I'm a spiritual seeker of sorts. I'm a scholar, or so I think. I'm a writer. I'm an avid outdoorsman. I'm physically and mentally and emotionally and spiritually fit, god damnit. But, am I not also a man? And doesn't a man have needs? Desires? Aspirations of the body? Doesn't a woman? And so isn't it natural for two creatures to spot each other across the watering hole, display their intentions, and steal away to meet among the secret trees? Was I going over there? Of course I was.

"OK, I'm going over there," I said.

"All right. I'm going back to the hostel," Scott said. "Don't forget we have an early train tomorrow. Have fun. Be careful. Use protection."

"Hello," Tia said, shaking her head from side to side. "You don't smoke, do you?"

"No," I said. "That's right."

"Thought not. I have to wait here for a few minutes until my manager lets me go. But you want to get a drink, right?"

"That sounds good," I said.

Minutes later we crossed the street and walked into

Johnny Foxes, an Irish pub on the frontage of River Ness. Yes, that's right, the river that flows from the famous Loch Ness through Inverness and six miles down to Moray Firth. You know that there is no Loch Ness monster, right? But apparently the Firth is swimming with bottlenose dolphins.

She ordered a Bailey's on ice, and ordered me a Guinness, both good Irish icons, and we sat in a booth near the window.

"You ever been to the festival in Edinburgh?" she asked.

"No," I said. "I keep hearing about it. Perhaps I should go. But I'm going to miss it, I think. We'll be gone before it starts up."

"I'm going up there in a couple weeks," she said. "I'm very excited. They have a drag show up there. All kinds of transvestites and transgendered people will be there. It will be the first time for me, so I'm very excited."

I nodded in agreement. "Sounds great," I said. And then, of course, Scott's voice came into my head—"She's probably a guy"—and yet, I had attended a drag show in the town where I live, The Kinsey Sicks. Best show I'd seen in years. I laughed and laughed. There was nothing odd about going to the festival for a drag show, was there? Perhaps it was the way she said the word "transgendered" that got up my back. Spooked me a little. Now I saw something in her face that I had not seen before, some square-ness in her jaw, some firmer construction in her complexion, some yang in her yin. She winked at me and bobbed her head back and forth.

"Where are you from?" I asked.

"Me? Well, I'm from Jordan. Amman actually. I grew up there. But my mom is Scottish. So I moved here, but it's so cold and rainy here. And people are not open-minded. I love the hot weather you know," she said. "Luuuve the sun. I love to lay-out in the sun and tan myself. Yes. But my doctor told me I could not be in the sun too much right now because of the hair removal treatment. Ooh, it hurts so much," she said. "It's like this burning pain every time. But I have to do it. It's like this," she said, and she pressed the back of her index finger into my arm. "It takes a little area like this, and it hurts so terribly."

"You're having a hair removal treatment," I repeated, as if I were the most dim-witted creature on earth.

"Yes. I'm removing the hair from all my body," she said. "You know," and she clicked her tongue three times against the roof of her mouth, "everywhere, including the secret places. The genitals," she whispered it. "And everywhere else too of course. Ooh, it hurts so much. But it's my dream."

So then, gentle reader, how long do you think it took me to see the picture clearly? But no, I was not yet convinced. After all, lots of women have hair removal treatments. The technology by which hair is removed was developed to cater primarily to women, was it not? The market for such treatments relies on women, does it not? No. There was nothing surprising about a Jordanian woman in Inverness undergoing a hair removal treatment.

"So you don't like it here in Inverness?" I asked.

"It's beautiful here if you like the rain and the clouds and the water," she said. "But I love the sun. I ache for the sun and to sun myself and tan my body. Oh, I love it too much. But here it is so dark and depressing to me. The worst part is not that, however" she said. "No. It's that people are not open-minded. So many people here are so critical and afraid. Maybe in a place like Glasgow or Edinburgh I would love it. I grew up in a city, you know. I love the city life. And people have so much experience and have seen so many things. Not like here in Inverness. These are country people who live in a very small world."

Have you not noticed, reader, how my little questions

lead to a great deal of unsolicited information?

"I have a friend," she said. "This friend is a transgendered person. She belongs to a very small group of us here in Inverness. Too few of us, really. And one night she came here to this pub, this very pub, with a man she had met, a man who was very excited to meet her." And she bobbed her head back and forth and clicked her tongue again. "They were sitting at the table over there, and talking, just like we are taking now. And then another man, a local man, a very ugly man who knew about my friend walked right up and said: 'This woman is a guy. Don't you know that, you fool. You're talking to a guy!' Ooh was she so mortified and embarrassed. So angry too. You can only imagine it. So now I am very curious about my rights under the law. How I am protected, and what I can do. You see, it is very hard for a transgendered person to live happily in Inverness."

I took up my glass and drank several swallows of the lovely Guinness. The air around us was delicate, and I was filled with the milk of human kindness. "So," I said, "you're a transgendered person."

"Oh yes," she said. "I am. But it has been such a long journey for me. Since I was 15, I knew I was a woman. And at that time, I started my journey. It took some time for my psychologist to confirm that I am sound in my mind. That I am not crazy. No. I am a very happy and stable person. Yes. And that took about one year. It was such a long year. After that I began my hormone therapy. Then I had my breast implants in Jordan." She removed the shirt she wore over her tank top to show me. She sat up very straight, her shoulders squared back. Nice work, I thought. "Yes, and in less than one year I will achieve my life's dream. I will be completely a woman."

Perhaps you are thinking what I'm thinking now, that line by Lady Macbeth: "Come, you spirits that tend on mortal thoughts, unsex me here!"

"You will have the surgery," I said.

"Right. That is the most important and delicate of all the transformations," she said. "I will have the surgery. It's not possible to find a doctor for this in Jordan. At least it is very dangerous, and maybe impossible. I had to come here to the UK to reach my dreams."

"I see," I said.

She drank the last of the Baileys over ice. She looked at me, harder now, and a measure of tension rose between us. She had just engendered me with the most fundamental part of her being, and held in trust this way, she waited to see if I was to violate it. I think she knew I would not. She also knew I was not attracted to her "romantically," and that tension fell away too. Something shifted between us. Was this friendship or fellowship? Neighborliness or cordiality? Or was it something else? Something without a name.

"That sounds wonderful," I said, words failing me. "I mean that you will be able to reach your dream. Most people don't, you know."

"Yes, of course it is," she said. "It is. It is so wonderful. I am so excited by it. And you see it's not this way with all transgendered people, because I can so easily pass as a woman, right? You didn't know, right? Some of my friends however will never be able to pass as a woman like me, but somehow I can do it. They will be forever stuck in between, and that is a very hard life for them. Yes. People will always look at them strangely, except other transgendered people. People will always hate them, and some people even feel violence toward them. Toward us. But for me, after I have the surgery, I think I will be completely a woman, and that is my dream since I was only 15."

Dear reader, have you read your Shakespeare lately? Do you remember your *Macbeth*? How strangely that play is consumed with lines devoted to gender—can you imagine it? Meeting Tia here in the very town black Macbeth murders his king and steals the throne? For example: there are these obvious lines given to Banquo, who addresses the witches: "You should be women, And yet your beards forbid me to interpret That you are so" (I.iii.45-47). That aside, do not forget that Lady Macbeth challenges Macbeth's manhood when he first refuses to murder his king. "I dare do all that may become a man; Who dares do more is none" (I.vii.46-47), he tells her. "When you durst do it, then you were a man," she tells him (I.vii.49). Of course, he does "durst do it," and in doing so, is not a man at all. I mean that the murder reduces him, as he foretells, and he becomes something else, a beast really, the rugged Russian bear, the armed rhinoceros, the Hyrcan tiger. When Lady Macbeth finishes her rant, she claims that at least she possesses a man's murderous powers, that she could dash the brains out of even her own child. To which, Macbeth exclaims: "Bring forth men-children only! For thy undaunted mettle should compose Nothing but males." (I.vii 73-75). Well, we know they both get it wrong. A man is not so murderous, at least not *only* so murderous—indeed, Duncan, upon greeting his Thanes after the war, is more motherly than fatherly, like a woman giving birth to these noble sons of Scotland: "Welcome hither! I have begun to plant thee, and will labor To make thee full of growing" (I.iv.28-30). Did you notice the pun on the word "labor," and that "growing" is about fecundity in the garden, about pregnancy? Later, MacDuff redeems all men when he reveals his wounded heart. Upon hearing that his entire family, his wife and children, have been murdered by Macbeth, Malcolm tells him: "Dispute it like a man." To which he responds, "I shall do so; but I must also feel it as a man" (IV.iii.219-221).

If Shakespeare wasn't Christian (for who can say what genius is), at least his plays live in a Christian world. And the Christian world, despite its present fear and paranoia on the issue of same-sex marriage, is a world founded on the "androgyny of primordial man." In *Genesis*, Eve is created of Adam, woman is formed of man, which points toward a relatively widespread belief (not to mention the origin of the incest taboo) that "human perfection, identified in the mythical ancestor, comprises a unity that is at the same time a *totality*," is how Eliade puts it in the first volume of his *A History of Religious Ideas*. "We should note," he continues, "that human androgyny has as its model divine bisexuality, a concept shared by a number of cultures." In this spirit, it is the androgyny who is whole, not the man alone or the woman, or even the man and woman in holy union. The androgyny is holy union. As you won't be stymied by another leap of faith, let's quote the *Tao*:

> Know the male,
> Yet keep to the female;
> Receive the world in your arms. (28, lines 1-3)

Inverness is home to an odd curfew law. At midnight the doors of all drinking establishments close. The drinking goes on inside for several more hours, of course, but the doors are locked tight. You must enter your place of choice before midnight, and when you decide to step out, there is no stepping back in.

"I need a fag," Tia said, bobbing her head from side to side.

"All right," I said. "I'll go out with you."

"We won't be able to come back in," she said.

"Right," I said. "That's all right. I've got an early train to catch."

I stood with her on the patio near the river front while she smoked. "It was lovely talking with you," she said. "I hope you have good travels."

"And you," I said. "And take care of yourself."

"Yes, of course," she said.

"I'm headed this way," I said, motioning up river.

"I'm headed that way," she said, motioning down river.

And from here, gentle reader, our scene becomes so filled with mist, it's impossible to know what happened next.

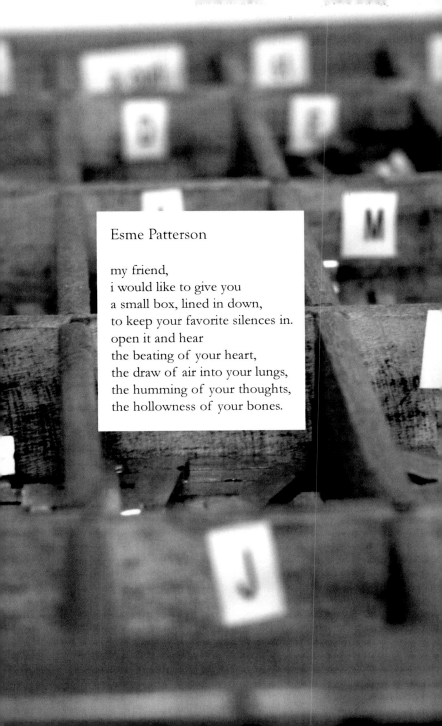

Esme Patterson

my friend,
i would like to give you
a small box, lined in down,
to keep your favorite silences in.
open it and hear
the beating of your heart,
the draw of air into your lungs,
the humming of your thoughts,
the hollowness of your bones.

Ryan Kerr

Ink

When I was printing one of my poems,
the paper jammed and each word
came out affixed on top of the others
in a mad, black puddle, the shores

     of which are random smatterings of thought

     ebbing off of the page and waning again
     back into the pool. There is enough ink
     there for me to pull the same words back
     out and place them perfectly as they
     were meant to be. But there is something

     so arresting in what has happened here by
     chance that I instead leave it as it is and
     stare at it for hours over months, picking

and prodding at the ephemeral thing,
wishing that all of my poems looked the same.

Jessica Baron

Regardless

all sort of things think about how
scholars label

African Byzantine
mentally lost perspective

counter approach it
ways in which crux

equation reversed constrained within
text insisting

the fourth experience
building blocks logic games

define content
pick one outcome

form as a problem how do you write
generative new form

whether you see black mountain
small magazines terms

shifts and disruptions pointing arrows

WORLD'S
SMALLEST
FEMUR

Fiction by Dawn Dennison

I n a small town with a parade for everything, Eldon Oster is known as the bone man. Eldon parades every Fourth of July, County Fair, Cherry Blossom Day, Old-Timers Day, and every Fall Fiesta. He carries in his outstretched hand a small glass spice jar with a cork lid. Inside the jar, held upright between two stiff strips of clear packing tape is a tiny bone, the length of a man's thumbnail. It is possibly the world's smallest femur, or so says the little index card Eldon holds above the jar.

Eldon has paraded his femur for going on ten years. He walks bowlegged down Main Street in a starched, white, long-sleeved dress shirt and a pair of brand new Wrangler's, their factory-folded creases running straight lines down the fronts of his legs.

He zigzags from one side of the street to the other, holding out the jar, and letting people look for as long as they like. He moves on when he gets the nod, the same nod people give a waiter when they've had enough fresh ground pepper. And though most people stand up to take a closer look at the femur when he passes by, Eldon will bend down to accommodate small children and pregnant women.

People guess at what animal the femur came from. Eldon has never attempted to find out. He hears fathers tell their children "That's the leg bone from a baby field mouse." Or "That's a lizard's back leg." Eldon neither supports nor disputes their theories.

When he is not parading, he keeps his femur in the medicine cabinet, behind the mirror in his bathroom. It is there because he likes to know it's just under his face while he shaves or brushes his teeth. Ten years earlier he'd found it in the impression his face made in the dirt, after he'd lain on the ground in a tin-foil sleeping bag while the Independence Creek Fire burned over him.

Before deploying a fire shelter, if you have time, dig out a shallow hole for your nose and mouth. This provides breathing room. Your face must remain pressed into the dirt until the fire passes over you. This protects your lungs, which can easily burn up from the super-heated air. You are far more likely to be killed from breathing this hot air than you are by direct flame contact.

-Fireline Handbook, revised, January 1988

Eldon and his crew were three days into a forest service deployment on a hot day in early August, 1990. They were descending a ridge and looking for hot spots when the wind picked up and bore down on them from the North. The crew boss radioed to the incident commander that the wind had re-ignited several of the hot spots and Eldon and the rest of the crew began to cut a line around these new fires. The wind shifted again, and the crew boss yelled, "Deploy! Deploy! Deploy!" Eldon recalled that the only time he'd ever heard this word used in such a way was during training exercises.

Thoughts of training exercises somehow calmed Eldon a little, and he had time to dig out some breathing room with the heel of his boot before he dropped to his knees and propelled himself forward, flat and face-down on the ground. His face sought out the indentation he'd just made with his boot at he pulled the shelter over himself and tucked it under his legs, his knees and hips. He jutted his elbows out from his sides, like a chicken, to pull out the slack and keep it off his back and shoulders. Viewed from the top, his deployed shelter looked like a rectangular Jiffy Pop popcorn maker, ready to be ripped open and devoured.

In the Fire Shelter Expect:
• Extremely heavy ember showers.
• Superheated air blast to hit before the flame front hits.

• Noise and turbulent powerful winds hitting the fire shelter.
　• Pin holes in the fire shelter that allow fire glow inside.
　　• Heat inside the shelter = Extreme heat outside
　　　-*Fireline Handbook*, revised January 1988

When Eldon and his crew saw that there was no way out, he found himself frozen for a moment, watching the others pull plastic-encased, accordion-folded shelters from the pouches that hung on the outside of their backpacks. He never thought he'd see the scene that was being played out on that smoky hillside. Eldon's shelter pouch was on the right side of the pack, at his hipbone. It said "fire shelter" in big black letters. He'd never used it, but he saw those words every time his eyes fell to the right and down. He sometimes rested his hand there, casually, yet protectively, the same way a pregnant woman rests her hand on her stomach.

As he snapped into action and tore open the plastic to get to the shelter, Eldon fought the urge to laugh, and knew that if he did, it would sound crazy and high-pitched; a hyena's laugh. He realized as he kicked at the dirt with his boot heel to form a small place for his face, that he had been watching himself, his own shaking hands were unfurling the shelter while he dug into his backpack to retrieve one of the four water bottles that he carried inside. It seemed to take forever by the time he threw his pack away from his deployment site and dove. Once he was down, it took another eternity to convince himself that his shelter was securely wrapped around him. When he thinks back to it realistically, the whole thing probably took forty seconds.

After each parade, Eldon walks back to his truck and places the jar on his dashboard, a bony little saint to guide him home. He marvels at its balancing powers. It always remains upright, even around the sharp turn out by the cement factory. To his right, on the passenger side floorboard is his dog, a wiry old blue heeler named Meg. She does everything with him, except the parade. Eldon always parades alone.

Later, when Meg and Eldon get home, he will drink four shots of Maker's Mark while he sits on his porch, the bone in the jar on the railing. He will fall asleep in the metal chair, and after a few hours will make his way into his little house and his single bed in the room off the kitchen. He only drinks after a parade, and parade nights mark the rare occasions when he gets a good night's sleep.

> Fire shelters should only be used in
> emergency situations, as a last resort.
> -*Fireline Handbook*, revised January 1988

When he was down, and encased in the shelter, he wished he'd said something to someone else. He wished he'd made a final contact. He wondered if any parts of the shelter were touching his body. The places where it touched were where he'd get burned the worst. He wished his radio weren't still in his backpack.

Inside the shelter it was dark, dark as a cast-iron woodstove. The kind of dark that magnified the noise of the fire; a sound that's often described as being under a freight train. Eldon always thought this was a cliché until he actually heard it. As he lay there with his face in the dirt he could almost see the grate and the black engine bearing down. It sounded like it was picking up speed as it rolled toward him. His instincts told him to run. In that instant, the act of lying down required more muscle than anything Eldon would ever do again. And even though they told him in fire school that staying in the shelter is the only thing that can save you, he felt like he was drowning—that same fight for air and life.

The roar of a wild land fire comes from the weather inside it. The flames don't make a sound. The noise comes from the tornado within the fire. When it was still a ways away, Eldon heard the man to his right reciting the Lord's Prayer. Soon it grew to a chorus of prayer, said louder every round, yet every round harder to hear. Eldon found himself yelling along with the others, until the sound of the fire drowned out everything, and he was left to mutter in the dirt, holding down the shelter on top of him while the fire roared over like an ocean.

Eldon doesn't really like parades, but more, he doesn't like to talk about the fire. He has a new job now, with a local tow truck company, and since he doesn't have a family, he put himself on-call 24 hours, seven days a week. He'll fudge the mileage for those who don't have insurance, and for a dead battery, Eldon will drive his own truck to you, and not charge a thing. He donates some time to the Senior Hikers, leading snowshoe trips and wildflower walks for the area's senior citizens. People who hike with him say that those guided trips are the most anyone's ever heard him speak. He is only thirty but looks fifty. His hair had turned white by the time he came home from the hospital. People know the story from the paper, and from the other crews who were there that day. No one asks about the fire anymore. No one's ever asked about the bone.

Flame contact can also cause the aluminum-foil layer to melt. Aluminum melts at 1,200 °F. Temperatures of flames in wildland fires average about 1,200 °F.
-*Fireline Handbook*, revised 1988

When it was over, when it grew quiet, Eldon sobbed into the ground, still flat out in the shelter. It was hard to imagine that this mournful death cry was coming out of him. He would pull a muscle in his shoulder from the heaving cries his body could not control.

They say you should wait at least 20 minutes after the fire passes, before you get out of your shelter—in case there's a flare-up. He called out to the others as he lay there spitting dirt and tears. He waited for his boss to shout the all clear. And after what seemed like hours had passed, Eldon lifted a corner of his shelter and peeked out.

The first thing he saw, when he finally rolled over on his back to glimpse the newly scorched world, was the giant boulder that had split the fire in two as it rushed over him. He doesn't remember it when he was setting up his shelter. He doesn't believe it was there before. The earth as far as he could see was black and steaming, with little pockets here and there of red and gray. His crewmates were still in their shelters. The silver turned to black and all of them seemed very small. From one curled up pile he could make out a boot and a leg bone.

He walked from pile to pile, four in all. Four piles of white teeth grinning, two still wearing helmets. He thought, wasn't it was the smoke that was supposed to kill us?

It was after the forest service helicoptered the bodies off the mountain, and after he'd been released from the hospital with minor burns on the backs of his legs and buttocks, after the memorial service and the planting of the crosses to mark the spots where the others had dted, Eldon hiked back up to the ridge and found where he'd lain face down, praying into the dirt. It was early spring. As he ran his fingers through the shallow hole that had saved him, he came up with the tiny white bone. He took out his pocketknife and dug around for the rest of whatever animal the bone had come from, but found nothing more.

He kicked out a hollow in the dirt and lay down again, this time with the back of his head in the ground instead of his face. He placed the small bone on his chest and looked up through bare branches into the morning blue sky. The world on that hillside was still mostly black. He stayed there until he saw four signs of life. There were pine drops growing out of the duff under the tree to his right, and a crow flew over. He ran his hand over the short new grass that was rising out of the ashen earth around him. Finally, just as the sun set, Eldon held up his own hand and let the sun silhouette it. Then he put the bone in his shirt pocket and headed down.

Brian Dickson

Summer Equinox

The strawberries have had their reach,
pinned to the soil underneath white gauze.

Morning, robins their fill, fire breasts bulged
with sweet grief.

There's no desperate road here, the game called
on a gust of rain, slant dance

glancing off the egg and spoon rushed
to female partners, fertility rights in tow

at a pagan festival. Drenched folks
stoked with wet arrival.

The eggs tilt
on the utensils, jostling with time

and dormancy, the hatched plan.
Broiler chickens weighed

in before dreary, but they know
ticking, and calm when

the cleaver comes. Look!
Day lilies emerge from the shells

with narcissus on their minds,
rippled pools at the ready.

We swim for joy, plenty of Dumpty's men
in our pockets, clamor to wash

their hands in the golden sap for lack of repair.
We peer into puddles, our reflections

smudge the mosquito larvae writhing
on brown shards.

The last male robin, juvenile, spring,
waits as the celebration disperses,

hauling the final seconds
in the waxing dusk.

Letter from a Biographer

Fiction by Erzsebet Gilbert
(formerly Elizabeth Johanna Gilbert)

To my most eminent subject,

I shall commence this message with a most sincere apology: I do beg your forgiveness as regards the tale of the eagle, the silken rope, and the box of matches. In retrospect, such storytelling would seem to indicate on my part some latent flicker of whimsy and an impulse toward (of all odious things) fiction, though in all fairness I would not go so far as to paint myself a liar. Having dispensed with such distasteful topics, however, I should like to request that you cease your unduly brutal condemnation of my work. I do so not so much for the sake of my own ego (already I feel myself secure in the knowledge of my own superb skills with grammar and mandolins, my admirable wit and moreover my impeccable taste in boots); rather, I fear for my reputation among the *community* of biographers as a whole.

My colleagues, indeed, expressed much arsenic-tinged envy at my attainment of you as my subject, given your illustrious achievements and the aurora of excitement surrounding your life thus far. Let me be the first to inform you (though surely you do not remain entirely unaware) that it is not every summer's morn that a biographer may examine such a fascinating person as yourself while enjoying nectar and melba toast. It is thus with immense perplexity that I have learned of your disgust at my portrayal of your lush, nay, Amazonian history.

For example, I cannot divine what flaw you find in my depiction of your childhood. Was I so grossly in error to describe your birthplace as "a pleasure-dome of the backwater, heavy with the reek of woodsmoke and wildcat musk, resonant with the amorous barks of moths" (page 119)? I can assure you I paid visit to your own native archipelago, even sampling the local pastries of dubious dough and documenting those sites where latitude and longitude fail to intersect. Perhaps it is my version of the rather sordid episode of the yellow stockings in which you find fault, but a brief investigation shall prove that I did indeed interview the gravedigger (*ad nauseam* and *requiescat in pace*), who affirmed that those inky asterisks are undeniably your youthful footprints (dare I say *footnotes*?).

You have branded me "a disgraceful fishmonger of the slimy salmon of deceit," (October 10th, Tuesday), and such comments have hardly escaped the attention of certain biographical authorities. Yet such a smear in all honesty astounds me, I the author of such classics as *Huang He: Beijing's Watchmaker of the Maniacal*, and *Cupid: The Missing Years*. How, pray tell, am I mistaken in asserting that your landmark decoding of the Mandeville hieroglyphs, as inscribed upon the inside of an ox's skull, arose not out of method but quite accidentally, inspired by a peculiar arrangement of twelve thimbles strewn across a floor? With all due respect, the notes of your assistants suggest otherwise. And if by some caprice of pixie or tectonic plate the maps I drafted as charting your course from Timbuktu to Goa have become somewhat inaccurate or physically impossible, please inform me as such and I shall issue a prompt correction. But still I must demand that you cease your unjust denunciation of my biographical endeavors as "the museum of a crafty charlatan."

You cannot, I would wager, imagine the sheer humiliation of standing before one's compatriot authors— before the likes of Madame Igazam van Nem herself, no less—to answer accusations so contemptible as those I face. Perhaps it has surprised you to learn that we biographers are no loose collection (an anthology, if you will) of sloppy spies or voyeurs peering lustfully through the peephole of the letter O. No, we are a venerable society of artists, those daring enough to take up our subjects not merely as a "career move," in vulgar parlance, but as a kind of immeasurable honor conferred upon us in the endless battle against grandfather clocks. We biographers write forever with the honesty of dove's quills, upon pages so brightly blank and objective as to flash signals across a lagoon at dusk. Therefore I ask you to empathize with the seasickness of my shame when I am forced to stand before our highest councils and defend myself against that most egregious of charges: *fiction*.

Not that I would wish to portray the biographical community as some totalitarian bloc of witch trials and their associated torches. We can actually be quite congenial and even boisterous, as is amply demonstrated by our custard festivals and the happily lewd acts committed on a number of solstices. Our laws and standards remain unspoken, though each of us knows the codes with that same intuitive morality that compels a stone to tumble towards soil and never the whistling mouth of the sky.

Still, I feel I may be pardoned for transgressing one of our lesser principles (for memoirists are another thing entirely, and may the Powers that Read shield me from that fate). Thus shall I offer to your steely gaze a bit of my own history. You may be interested to learn that I was a precocious infant whose intellect and swordsmanship surprised even my noble kin (prominent enough that I am certain the name requires no mention), and I never failed to startle my private tutor, a descendant of Archimedes given to bouts of ingenious amnesia. I did not, like some more barbaric sorts, stumble into my profession while wandering an academy's halls among pillars of chalkdust and fossilized philosophies. Nor did I take it up as some mere *job*. I knew from the very wellsprings of my literacy what art could be my singular calling.

Among our loftier circles, it is oft whispered that "one's name is not the beginning of one's table of contents." Scorning the jiggling, faddish tangos of analysis and reinterpretation, I take this to mean that for a faithful chronicler such as I, the self is never a subject of any substance at all. Any given *Homo sapiens* may well be considered the hero of its own grand narrative, but it is the blessing of the biographer to possess no story of which to speak. We are but the gatherers, diligent honeybees and scrupulous dormice, amassing the tales of other, more epic humans in order that they might not gust away in the sandstorms to come. Thus, though I happen to be a most gifted layer of bricks, a connoisseur of fine champagnes with phenomenally glamorous eyelashes and a matchless ability to seduce wolves, these details are of no matter. My duty is to Truth alone.

And so how can you contest my documentation of your various caterwauling romances: the shoemaker, the voluptuous housecat, the floutist carved from soap? It is probable, I suppose, that you might find the divulging of such facts—and I do believe we both know them to be so—something of an embarrassment. Nevertheless, it was I who unearthed, beneath a heap of erotic featherdusters and pillows deep as scarlet fevers, your lost verses and vows of love. If I may be so bold as to quote: "you, my darling landfill of all that is insignificant, you fill the dustpan of my pelvis with your glittering filth" (dated May 1st, year of rat). Thus do I believe that when I named the chimneysweep as most beloved to your innermost, fleshiest heart, I have departed not a whit from the integrity of my career.

In the interests of compromise, I concede that I may at times have embellished certain events, the "plot points" of your life, if you will, and it may be the case that some affairs were not so scandalous, some distances not so vast, some skies not so violet and so violent as I have portrayed them. But I promise that any such liberties on my part arise solely from my passion for you, my subject, though some of my fellow biographers may be incapable of understanding such a crystalline justification. As such, if a particular person did not in fact exist (in the material sense), or an occurrence did not take place (in the paltry five senses), or a certain sentence did not spill as absinthe off your tongue, one might accept these matters as a breed of fact in themselves, inasmuch as fervor is never fiction.

Were you only to agree to meet with me for an evening of waltzing and fabricated starlight, we might sort through what I feel to be a simple misunderstanding. Alas, you have declined all seven of my previous messenger pigeons, in spite of the fact that my feet are better suited for dancing than those of any tarantula. My offer still stands, nonetheless, and I shall wait as scheduled at the flanks of the marble horse.

I can only hope that you will see Reason's wondrous will o' the wisp, and step before the community of the biographers to pardon me and revoke your cruel remarks. In the meantime (and time is forever too mean), I shall return to my latest project, an as-yet-untitled account of the tumultuous marriage between the nineteenth duke of Venice and the Adriatic Sea. And I shall close my plea by counseling you to examine closely a mirror, or the blue mantle of a standing pool. You may find, upon careful scrutiny, that I was undeniably correct in writing of your face as a near-perfect mimicry of the August moon, and see most clearly the truths that I have put to press.

With utmost humility, I remain,

Your Biographer

> Postscript. If all along it has been the fear of legal retribution that has blared loudest in your mind, let me take this opportunity to assure you that, as regards the Greenland incident, I have confirmed that the statute of limitations on arson does not exceed eleven years.

Matterdaily.org is a news, views & information website run by staff and volunteers of Wolverine Farm Publishing with the intent of making Fort Collins and Northern Colorado better places to live.

The news is free, ask at any street corner, bar, library. Investigating, compiling, writing, and reporting it is not. We need your help.

SUPPORT LOCAL MEDIA.

WRITE WHAT YOU KNOW.

WWW.MATTERDAILY.ORG

Susan Tepper

Under the Avocet Feathers

Lucy is the side of me sitting under a sun umbrella
scratching at a keyboard missing
the escape key sipping a chai tea latte

Pan is the side admiring the nomad teen jangling
his tin cup at the wary weekenders singing
to a bluegrass banjo only he can hear

she says let's walk the savannah—no *strut*—
let's show off our bipedal knees and our swivel hips
cover up grab a tool and start scheming dinner

he says there's more to me than knees
a goat romping chomping wild onion
bleating boorishly in a dandelion lea

standing atop a cliff she strings teeth
on an animal ligament accessorizing
tattooing herself with red ochre

hiding in the sagebrush below he giggles
madly throwing rocks at her yelling
get over yourself

she screams that he can figure out fire
on his own tonight retreating
into the comfort of ingenuity

but the echoes die in an oasis in the ahaggar mountains
and they will reconcile before slipping
quietly under a quilt

of avocet feathers

Family

Business

Non-Fiction by Blair Oliver

When the fog lifted I saw my boy mucking about the shore, sweeping his orange aquarium net through the shin-deep water. The evening before, we'd hunted bugs beneath the lily pads and rocks. Frogs had slipped from the pads. Sometimes, this was accompanied by the crash of bass. The moon had waned, reclined in a hammock of stars, and we'd bottled a boatman, three baetis, and a spider.

Now, I was clear across the lake in a leaky rowboat, my fly rod bent like a cane. A smallmouth had swallowed my popper and made a cat's cradle of my line through the deadfall. The fish was still on, though, and I was ready to dive in after it. Water was rising around my shins, too. I scanned the shell of woods beyond my boy and saw no sign of my wife or daughter. Owen must've dropped from bed while they were still asleep in the cabin and tottered outside to join me. I wondered how long a full diaper could keep him afloat. I imagined he'd be better off raised by the bears.

"Son," I shouted.

He raised his net overhead. It burned like a torch in the dawn. At two, he was liberty itself, though I didn't think Jennifer would've seen it that way had she come outside to find me wrestling with a bass as the boy was left to exercise the freedom of youth in the lake. It wouldn't matter that I'd left the kids with her. I was fishing, which to the unconverted is somehow less important than safety or sleep.

I yelled for him to stay put. He stepped forward, then thought better of it and retreated. He did this several more times, thin legs racing like a sandpiper's in the ebb and flow of beach combers. I grew up on the ocean, even if my own father didn't include me in his fishing.

The old boy used to keep dart guns to shoot the garden spiders that had crept indoors. He didn't teach me how to fish, but he gave me my own gun, and when he was home we sneaked around corners, orange suction cups raised as

he whistled the tune of Mutual of Omaha's *Wild Kingdom.* My father would call himself Marlin Perkins while I was always Jim and the men. We'd make a mess of the walls until my mother appeared, disarmed us, and sent me to my room so she could have a word with my father. I sat on the floor outside of their room, frightened with guilt. I'd rather have a thousand times gotten spanked than have them fight again. The first sign of adulthood is realizing you're not responsible for your parents' arguments, that they too have lives of their own. Sometimes I wonder if I'll ever get to this point.

Jennifer and I had done our own arguing, including the night before. I wasn't always as decent as I should've been. Lately, I've started seeing my father in the mirror. Everyone knows this is the first sign of old age. Emails to old girlfriends don't help. One asked if I was thinking outside my box. "I'm shy," she said, "but I have the imagination of ten thousand injuns." When I told my father I was going to school to study poetry he said, "You're not getting funny on me, are you?"

Owen was watching me from the shore. I leaned over the gunwale, nearly capsizing the boat, gripped my line close to the sunken wood and broke off the fish. I knew from my own flashes of sudden memory children were born old enough to remember these fights and flights. We press so hard to avoid the mistakes our parents made we walk blindly into ones of our own. Owen didn't have a dart gun; he made sure we punctured holes in the lid of our bug jar. I released my rod to the puddle at my feet and coerced the boat around with the oars. The old boat never liked me. She groaned as I leaned into the wood and zigzagged toward home.

Owen's net was littered with life. Pale green nymphs curled and twisted in the basket. He jumped up and down, clearly ready for his first fish. Teaching your child to fish isn't like teaching him to run the family business. The stakes are much higher than that. After killing spiders, my father taught me the proper way to carry a refrigerator into the house. He sat on the stoop, wiped his brow and said, "Remember, Blair, I'll always love your mother more than you. She came first." I nodded, then threw my shoulder into the refrigerator, hiding my face against the cold metal. The old boy left home soon after.

My daughter was two when she first helped me hook and land a rainbow from the neighborhood pond. Thereafter, she'd humored me once or twice by joining me on the couch to watch a fishing show on television, but she was soon using the rod I'd given her as a limbo stick.

Owen, to my immense satisfaction, had rescued the rod. He'd braved the blows of the girls. He didn't understand yet that he'd never again see the attention he now got from the neighborhood girls. Or maybe that was just my experience. I do know that as we exited a parking garage a few weeks back he stopped and pointed at a mural on the wall of an eagle buzzing a river.

"What's that birdy doing?" he'd said.

We were on the eagle-level of the garage! In the New West, bison graze alongside billboards of bison.

"He's fishing, son."

"Where's his fly rod?" Owen had asked, confirming I'd done something right.

On the lakeshore, I handed him the rod as I tied another garish, rubber-legged popper to the tippet. "Okay. I'm going to put this fly out there, and you're going to catch a fish." Who knew what else to say? We were too early for casting by the clock. The danger, I supposed, was pushing your kids too hard in your own directions, though I couldn't say I knew that from experience. Fathers and sons ought to forge rituals and traditions to bond them, even if those bonds are artificially generated. Even before we cast, I paused to gauge the light, the quality of the wind. Detail would be important. I just didn't know what that detail would be.

The popper was too big for the light leader I'd tied for spring midge fishing in the river. With the boat, I'd been able to get close to the structure and flop the fly overboard. I had to labor from shore to deliver the foam where we might attract a fish. This was sloppy business, devoid of the tight, graceful loops I'd hoped to model. I often spend days thinking of little else than fishing only to find myself too anxious or impatient to do it properly once those precious few hours have arrived. If I was going to teach my son how to fish, I was going to help him see that catching was only a part of it.

That would begin tomorrow.

In the meantime, we watched as the yellow popper sat just off the edge of the lily pads, forty feet out and down the muddy shoreline. Owen had dropped his net and held the rod with both hands. On his scale, a bluegill would be a salmon.

Nothing was happening. The sun was rising higher behind us, and soon the girls would wake and materialize from the woods. No doubt they would have something in store for us, like going to the wedding we were ostensibly at the lake for.

Kids, I thought, might actually require catching something when they fished, so I took the rod from Owen and twitched the popper. It skipped from the pads, and a small bass shot from the water. I set the hook, then offered back the rod. Owen went for his net instead.

"Good job, Daddy," my son said, which was the best music.

I reeled in the little fish and swung it over to Owen's net. This was a first, of sorts. Back arched, he held the net with both hands up and away from him as the fish wriggled in the webbing. I lowered the rod, grabbed the leader and began to raise the spiky green fish from the net. Owen hopped from one foot to the other. The fish cleared the net and I made to hand it to him. He pivoted and ran screaming up the bank.

"What's going on here?" Jennifer said, appearing with Fiona from the trees.

"The fish tried to lick me," Owen cried.

The girls folded their arms across their chests. Owen darted his tongue against his hand to demonstrate, then everyone turned to look at me.

Is it true that if we forgive our fathers there'll be nothing left?

Dona Stein

Dusk

We thought grown-ups were mean
didn't want us wild on the hill
where we chased cousins, pelting the boys

with pine cones and grabbing their shirts.
We didn't know those boys
would be men on sofas coughing, waiting

in dreams they can't escape. We hid,
shouted their names as we jumped
from behind white trees. We didn't know

we wanted to make day last longer,
not give in to the forgetfulness of sleep
as we ran from birch to pine

not answering calls from the house,
scent of sap strong in our throats,
hair flying, breathless

Slugs & Snails

Fiction & Drawings by
Sue Ring deRosset

Olivia smokes a joint at the kitchen table while I wash the dishes. Through the window I can see my adult son in the backyard, buzzed hair backlit by the sun. It is a late afternoon in July. Olivia says, "Look, Melissa, you've raised him well, you've taught him everything he needs to know." I turn to her, tasting the rise of bile in my gullet and wincing. "I told him about the birds and the bees," I tell my sister, "but not about the slugs and the snails."

My sister and I were born into a family of molluscicidal maniacs. On land or at sea, there was no snail that was safe in our presence, whether inside the brick garrisons of our gardens or beneath the snorkeling squadron of the Holt family on vacation in the Florida Keys. Our paternal great-grandfather, John Cotton Holt (one of the first deep-sea divers to use Cousteau's and Gagnan's new invention, the "Self-Contained Underwater Breathing Apparatus") hauled up, in 1944, the largest Giant clam ever taken from the South Pacific. One half of this white bivalve is on display among irises in a dappled alcove in Grandma's garden, and who knows where the other half landed. But for our generation the mollusk-killing mischief started when our father, a Naval officer, was stationed at NATO in 1970. Brussels was, for us girls at least, the first battleground of gastropod carnage in a war that grew gorier as we grew older.

One night when I was six and Olivia four, our well-meaning parents took their weird little daughters—we were clad in matching pastel "fruit" dresses, red kneesocks, and saddle-shoes, and sported page-boys with severely short bangs—to a restaurant near the Grande Place, to immerse us in a little Belgian culture. Mom said, "Most American kids will never get a chance like this!" Belgian culture, it turned out this time, did not involve a walking-tour past lace-makers who wore the traditional costume and tatted doilies in dark alcoves that smelled of furniture polish; it did not mean chasing pigeons across the thousand-year old cobblestones of the Grande Place; and most regrettably it had nothing to do with blissing out on smooth dark chocolate, each *bon-bon* melting with the next in a giant silky mass across our tongues.

Belgian culture on this particular evening meant *les escargots*. "Escargots" (pronounced "S-car-go!") was a deceptively benign and entertaining word until the cultural items to which it referred arrived in scooped platters, one to each cup. Olivia and I, tiny *hors d'oeuvre* forks in hand, looked to our parents after the platters arrived. *Snails?* This must be their idea of a sick joke.

"Go on, McFuzz, you'll like it," Dad assured me, then nodded at my little sister. "The Star-bellied Sneetch looks willing to try." (We were going through a Dr. Seuss phase and had insisted on these monikers.) I gave Dad a mean and suspicious look, then inspected my dinner. The cooked yard-critters glistened menacingly by candlelight. Greasy with butter and their own mucousy lipids, and recoiling from their brown shells, they'd expired with their thumbnail-shaped trapdoors extended as if in surrender, or supplication. I poked a snail with the fork and it bobbed and rolled, making a hollow *clonk* in its cup. Pulling a face, I sought empathy in The Sneetch, who tensed one corner of her mouth nearly to her chin. We set down our forks and enquired into the availability of *pommes frites* instead. But there would be no French fries tonight. It was *escargots* or go hungry. So, in the spirit of forced adventure, and in the interest of keeping a little babyfat on our bones through the interminable, peri-arctic, Belgian winter, we ate them.

After four years of gastrointestinal challenges, including but not limited to mussels, squid, eel, oysters, sweetbreads, and garden snails, Olivia and I somehow arrived safely back in the land of French fries, Cheez-Whiz, and Ding-Dongs. At once we were conscripted to fight Grandma Holt's battles against snails and slugs around her home in San Diego. Grandma wore muumuus and smoked Pall-Malls from an ivory cigarette-holder and only wore shoes at parties. She promised Olivia and me and our three cousins, the Baxter kids, that we could earn five cents a snail and ten cents a slug for each one we killed.

In Grandma's gardens grew the most enchanting plants. Tall palms waved their fronds like banners around her castle. Inside the stucco walls of The Compound flourished many brilliant flowers, larger-than-life: towering tropical ginger; flame-faced Birds of Paradise with leaves like lances; rows of irises and amaryllis like spectating duchesses; a profusion of roses, from yellow teacups on cagelike trellises to giant blood-red vulgar things drooping from thorny stems; hanging baskets of fuchsias hemorrhaging from their tutus; clay urns spilling over with geraniums; and staghorn ferns affixed to layers of peat moss, nailed to boards in the lath-house and crowned with banana peels. Crawling along the slatted roof of the lath-house, the jointed, alien appendages of a desert Night-blooming cereus fluttered a blossom or two like a monogrammed handkerchief every summer at midnight, wafting pheromones for a rare moth. There were hedges of nasty-tasting purple pucker-berries, and scratchy crab-grass lawns steaming with dog poo and bordered by bricks that stubbed our toes, and mature orange trees for climbing. Grandma's oranges balanced the Holt and Baxter kids's diets of scrambled-eggs-and-ketchup, doughnuts, corn *tortillas*, and *chile rellenos* and prevented scurvy in our ranks. Damp secret passageways led through maidenhair ferns and Virginia creeper to the stucco-walled front courtyard and the neighbor's rose gardens. Sprinklers erupted automatically in the wee morning hours, and legions of slugs and snails glided across every imaginable surface of Grandma's garden.

We three girls—Olivia, cousin Steph Baxter, and me—always arose earlier than did the boys, who stayed up late watching Madonna on MTV. This gave us a supreme advantage in the war against the mollusks. We sprang from our beds at the first intimation of grey dawn, ran down the stairs and outside, and fanned out across the sopping wet garden. We turned over the bricks that stubbed our toes, unfurled the giant ginger leaves, peered behind the dog's water bowl and under great-grandfather's Giant half-clam and along the stucco walls and in the damp woodruff and moss by the hose spigot, and, one by one, we plucked the snails from their hiding places with a delicate popping sound as their suction gave way to our tugs. But, early in the morning, we often did not have to look even that hard. For the audacious snails and slugs would be trailing their slime out in the open, across the porch steps, walkways, and lawns. We collected hundreds, *thousands*, of mollusks. All summer, every morning, we crept through the garden, careful in the placement of our bare feet, fingers hovering low over the leaves. Stephanie and Olivia drifted like faerie folk or ghostly damsels through the pearly fog, pale and innocuous and silent; as if they were only picking buds and blossoms, or tasty ripe berries.

I have not said yet what we did to all those poor creatures; it is not an easy thing to confess. But it's part of my story, part of who I am, and it's important that you know this about me. So. We killed them. We used two of the bigger, heavier garden-border bricks and named the slaughterhouse corner of Grandma's *Better Homes & Gardens* award-winning yard "The Abattoir." We piled our collections in great clicking heaps beside the two bricks, each of us calculating our salaries—(# Snails x 5¢) + (# Slugs x 10¢)—and then somebody would have to do the grisly deed before the gastropods threw back their opercula and slimed away, trailing nickels and dimes in strings of mucus back to their hiding places.

We worked shifts at The Abattoir. The Squasher had to shove a writhing pile of gastropods onto the bottom brick, then bring the top brick down on them, stand on it, jump up and down on it. The snail-shells cracked and crunched. Then we had to ascertain we'd killed them all. Peeling the top brick like a slice of bread off a peanut butter sandwich, we were always disgusted by the sight: A muscular, grey, giant silky mass coalesced and contracted in on itself; it was a horrid, snot-colored, moving goo mixed with pieces of brown striped shell. The animals weren't individuals anymore. We dug shallow graves and buried them en masse.

Grandma often awoke early to join the massacres. In a muumuu the color of parrots, smoking her first Pall-Mall of the day, and shoeless like the rest of us, Grandma stomped around the yard and squashed snails and slugs with her bare callused feet. Along all the brick paths and flagstone meanders and across the patio lay flattened blobs that dried brown and crispy when the fog burned off and the summer sun came out and broiled them in their own grease. We didn't like Grandma coming out to help us; the more snails and slugs she murdered, the fewer available to the five of us, which meant less money to be made that summer.

No matter where Dad got stationed—Virginia, California, Rhode Island—we always spent summers at Grandma Holt's, killing snails and slugs in the mornings and boogie-boarding with our cousins in the afternoons. Spring breaks, however, presented yet other opportunities for our family to engage in creative snail-killing ventures.

Our maternal grandparents lived in Florida. They kept fins, snorkels, and masks in their ultra-tidy garage and loaned Mom and Dad their white leather-seated Cadillac sedan that smelled like Armour-all. The four of us drove down to the Keys to—you guessed it—hunt conchs and other shell-bearing creatures. We snorkeled in warm shallow water over hills of undulating eelgrass, watching for the bayonnet glint of a barracuda's approach, and we kidnapped living mollusks from their rightful habitat and paddled them to shore. We stacked them in buckets, where they died in the hot trunk on the way home. Back at the grandparents's place, Mom and Dad buried the stinking creatures in ant-hills or clothespinned their muscular feet to vinyl lines until the shells were either skeletalized by the insects or released with a nauseating thump to the ground. The seashells turned out clean and glassy and smelling only of the sea, while on the clothesline remained sinewy strips of conch jerky, covered with flies. (And thank heavens for those flies; otherwise, we might've been forced to eat the jerky.)

Year after year of Spring vacations "shelling" and summer mornings at Grandma's spent killing gentle garden creatures eventually exacted a moral toll on my sister and me. Why I did what I did, I can hardly fathom now. The easy answer is to leave it at that: I was a child, I didn't know what I was doing, I didn't know I could have chosen the path of the conscientious objector. But the difficult truth is that I did know what I was doing, and though I suffered the quease from violating my conscience, I went on collecting living seashells and getting handsomely paid to squash snails and slugs, for some five or eight years. Also there was the allure of approval, the collector's gratification of finding and cataloguing rare seashells, the desire to feel helpful and beneficial to the adults, the loyalty in protecting Grandma's enchanted garden from enemies, and the siren-song of peer pressure. We girls were competing against our male cousins, who awoke around the crack of noon and poked around the sunny yard looking for a snail to kill. It was our intention that they'd never find a one. This was both a job and a game at which we could win. But mostly, I'm now ashamed to admit, it was just greed.

And we made a killing. But every time I brought that

massive abattoir brick down on another writhing mass of animals, I'd feel a pinching squeeze to the ethical gland in my brain: Someday I'd pay for my mercenary cruelties. Looking back, I feel as if it were not I who ate the garden snails in melted butter (and swallowed), not I who stole beautiful sea-animals (only minding their own business) from Atlantic beds of eelgrass, not I who did such terrible things to thousands of sentient animals in our grandmother's lush coastal gardens.

On earthly scales both small and large, how we humans have crafted a thousand hells from one shared heaven. It feels strange to reflect on that first summer we were drafted to kill snails and slugs because far, far away, beyond the purse-string borders of my awareness, a larger and most terrible war was raging, crushing human beings on both sides even as it was winding down. One night in the summer of '75—Olivia, Steph, and I were all presumed asleep in our beds, the boys I guess were watching TV in the den—some guests arrived at my grandmother's front door. Above our whispers and giggles the doorbell buzzed and the dogs barked. We shushed ourselves to hear the murmur of unfamiliar voices moving into the livingroom. We crept down the hall in our nighties and sat on the staircase landing, toes curling over a carpeted step: We were out of sight, but perfectly able to hear everything.

Some Navy pilots had finally been rescued from POW camps and had come home. One had spent seven or eight years along the Red River near Hanoi; he'd been shot down early on in the conflict. The pilots were either friends of Grandma's late husband, or Pensicola pals of our dad's or uncle's, or Naval Academy colleagues of close friends of the family. We heard Dad mixing them drinks in glass tumblers at the dry bar. Whenever someone took a sip, you could hear the ice cubes clinking, then settling again.

The ones with unfamiliar voices sounded tired. Their voices were different in other ways as well. All of the adults in our family were strong and adventurous, confident almost to the point of arrogance, authoritative to be sure, and you could hear it in the way they spoke. "Up and at 'em, troops, let's get a move on!" they'd command, loading us into the station wagon for a trip to the PX. But these men, their voices were hesitant and shy, voices with feelers, utterances so soft we had to shut our eyes to hear them from the stair.

They spoke of morale and solitary confinement. They spoke of tapping messages to each other across the damp stone walls in Morse, and leaving small notes in the latrine, and how even the smallest sign of camaraderie could lift the spirits. When they said *the rats were big, scary fuckers*, we furtives on the step unhinged our jaws and glanced at each other in shock, and Olivia whispered, "He said a naughty word." The men spoke of upholding the code—ever only giving their names, dates of birth, and serial numbers—no matter how bad it got. They spoke of the spiritual strength found in family, God, and country. Then one of them said that often he'd gotten so hungry he licked the maggots from his wounds and ate them for the protein.

"*Maggots!*" I said, then clamped a hand over my mouth.

"Shh!" Steph whispered, bugging her eyes at me. Silence fell over the company in the livingroom. Olivia and I looked at each other, the same looks we'd thrown by candlelight at that Belgian restaurant four years earlier, the corner of her mouth dragging down in disgust.

Then footsteps in the foyer. Mom scowling from the bottom of the staircase: "Melissa Holt!—*Girls!*—What are you doing? Get back into bed. *This minute!*"

We scurried upstairs, shrieking and giggling.

"And I don't want to hear another *peep* out of you three!"

Once in bed, of course, we chickies peeped to each other, too softly to be heard from downstairs. I wondered how awful the maggots must've tasted. How the giant silky mass crawling across the back of the tongue and around the teeth and gums would've totally unnerved me. Distracted and repulsed by the idea of someone being forced to eat maggots, as we'd been forced to eat snails, it did not occur to me to ask until years later, *What wounds?* At the beach, by the pool, an ex-POW would take off his T-shirt and I'd notice a hitched knobby shoulder, or one arm dangling a bit shorter than the other, or a row of scars like flattened, shiny-pink slugs across a rail-thin back.

My sister and I, by the time we were entered high school, had begun to rebel against the annual garden-gastropod massacres. I'd had nightmares featuring The Abattoir and half-dead slugs screaming for mercy and snails with broken shells limping off into the fog to suffer and slowly die. And then our garden borders dissolved. We saw that the killing fields and abattoirs were everywhere, and that both sides always lost.

We carry the emotional scars, of course, of being made to do things we had not really wanted to do, and now I fear for my eighteen-year old who is shipping out tomorrow for Kabul. He is terrified and I don't know what to tell him. Hell, I'm terrified. From the kitchen window over the sink where I've just finished washing the dishes (barefooted, wearing a muumuu, and sharing Olivia's joint), I can see him, backlit in the garden, rescuing grasshoppers from the dog's water dish while the Golden retriever looks on and wags her tail. But there's another, weirder scar I carry, and I can't believe I'm going to even mention it, considering.

One summer when I was ten or eleven, I picked a snail off Grandma's porch step at dusk and held it aloft until it came out of its shell. I let it glide across my skin. Such a small and vulnerable creature, an architectural wonder spiraling in on itself to a peaked twirl on a domed roof. Its delicate, stalked eyes conducted a private silent orchestra. With curiosity, its feelers pawed the air, and its sticky muscular foot rippled and pushed and dragged across my fist. Then she lowered her face to the second joint of my right hand's middle finger, and bit me.

I am not imagining or inventing the snail attack—uh, retaliation. I've talked to a few biologists. Inside a snail's small, round mouth are radially-arranged rows of *radulae*, horny bands with toothlike structures, which she can extrude onto an edible surface, such as a leaf. But the biologists dismissed the snail bite as unlikely—its round mouth is too small to insuck even the tiniest tag of skin, it has no predilection toward carnivory, etc—but I tell you, this is how the insurgent invertebrate counted coup. And it hurt!—sharp and swift as a paper cut. Afterward, I bore a small, round lesion with tiny serrated edges, pink where my summer tan had been scraped off. I did not kill that snail— how could I have? Instead, I carried her to the shadowy alcove of Grandma's iris garden where half of the largest Giant clam in the world had come to rest. In the gloaming the air smelled of wet moss. My finger a ramp, I waited for the snail to slide off my fingernail and onto a leaf. Even today, thirty years later, I can point to a small white scar on my knuckle. You see?—It's right here.

Jared Schickling

Fort Collins Hotel / Cache

la poudre, this side of FRENCH
                              planets, undammed POO-DER you issue
                                        from mountain peaks fed
                                        each year into twister
                                                swept plains,
where the young girls' legs are
                              fatter you employ in conjunction
                                        w/ the corn brought in
                                        to GREELEY but here
hard
by your annual   where
ravishing thighs know not of their
                                        edge, into the salve

                                        would climb
                              continents to touch the source
                              texts along the bank WHEN
THE TRAPPERS' INJUN

                    POWDER WOULD KEEP LIKE HER WATERED-DOWN
                    TAB
                              ALL THROUGH A CERTAIN
                                        longest winter

Megan Guidarelli

Sin City

I desire the violent jolt of the capital
the ivory night. no sleep.
the pulsing bulbs—
piercing pupils.

Crashing, wrecking symphonies
hymns of aching sound—
the lullaby for those left over.

Missing identities lie in gutters
with spectacle frosted glasses
shaken not stirred

Celestial comets for dinner
and angel cake dessert
we wipe our haloed chins clean
and spit smoke through our teeth.

With pointed toes in rubber souls,
just know, there's no bounce back
after falling from this high.

No detachment to none of this.
Forever high,
I, peer to god

Paul DeHaven

Untitled

the sun lay its head down like a plane
for kings and pawns and the between
shined wearing whiteness.

god bless her brittle hands and god
bless the curse they carry.
she discovered the woods as gentleness
stepping upon its witness,
all made more well beneath the curious
pressing weightlessness.
she threaded the shadow by the light,
a bishop upon his own earth.

then sunsnow-
the coin overturned by
the hand that moves all things.

the straight made crooked;
crooked, straight.
the light made dark;
dark, light.

BE YOUR OWN

An *interview with*
Will Oldham
(Bonnie "Prince" Billy)
by Elliott Johnston

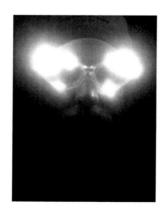

Will Oldham is supposedly a man of darkness. The character that emerges from press linked about the web is a mysterious and quiet soul hiding behind odd, royalty-evoking monikers like Palace, Palace Music, Palace Brothers and, since the late '90s, Bonnie "Prince" Billy.

Oldham's musical landscape is emotionally serrated. Its topography can be murderous, heart-achingly tender, joyous, sad, perverted, and uninhibited. He takes some textural cues from the warm rusticity of very old American folk and the freeform dirt of '80s indie-rock. Live, he often unbuttons the soft, brooding innards of his records. Wild, wooly, and shaggily-mustachioed, like a blonde Yosemite Sam grown to an average height, he yelps and howls over ramshackle country rock.

He is known for shunning the music-industry-as-usual. He tours when and how he feels like it. He books shows in non-major-markets like Laramie, Wyoming, or non-traditional venues like churches and record shops, or simply around good camping spots. He records often — in different locales with a revolving cast of conspirators. Most songs are recorded in just a few takes. Compared to other artists, he rarely gives interviews. Music journalists, when they do get access, often color over cryptic answers with adjective-heavy character sketches: backwoods solipsist, recluse, nomad.

"I See a Darkness" is perhaps Oldham's best-known song. The track, with its protagonist, who exposes bleak visions like he's expelling demons from his chest, was covered by The Man in Black, Johnny Cash, in 2000 (with Oldham singing backup). Cash, of course, added certifiable American mythology to an already heroically brutal song.

But, Oldham's output cannot be defined by darkness alone. Perhaps like no other contemporary, he has persistently taken new chances while putting out consistently great work. His recent albums *The Letting Go* and *Lie Down in the Light*, have meditated more on love, communal joy, and inner peace than ever before, but, characteristically, there is a tack on the chair: even a good day has awkward happenstance, even love illuminates humiliating urges. He's also shown spontaneity and a diverse palate through cover songs. Though the picks sometimes read like jokes — Mariah Carey, R. Kelly, Danzig — through speakers, Oldham digs up the profound.

Matter Journal spoke with Oldham over the phone in the spring of '08 after the release of *Lie Down in the Light*[1], on Chicago-based independent label Drag City Records. From his home in Louisville, Kentucky, he talked about navigating the seas of light and darkness, finding wisdom through song, and how his princely persona is designed for heroic acts.

Matter Journal: Some of the *Lie Down in the Light* songs are fighting for a more hopeful perspective in the lyrical content than your songs used to. I get this idea that it might have, at least in the past, sometimes been easier to be bleak, and that to look on the positive side of things, maybe, takes more energy.

Will Oldham: It always takes energy to turn an idea into music, and keep it from being just the idea. The goal inherent in the effort to make the music is an optimism, whether or not there is some kind of superficial bleakness or darkness. The very idea of expending creative energy, financial energy, time, on these things implies that there is something worthwhile about it all.

And the truth is, the default or the easy thing, if you relax into it, is darkness. And sometimes, the easy thing is light and positivity. Trying to bend over backwards and

1 This March, Oldham released *Beware*, his eighth full-length album as Bonnie "Prince" Billy. It isn't available at press time, but Drag City is billing it thusly: "Though *Beware* shares spit with its immediate predecessor released this past summer, *Lie Down in the Light*, its reach is longer and stronger, more grandiose."

kill yourself to create something that just isn't part of your world at that moment seems detrimental because during all that time of too much labor, you are not communicating. And to me, the main point is to communicate as often as possible, as deeply as possible, and as much as possible.

MJ: I was listening to a Nick Cave interview and he said something along the same lines. He was reacting to this idea that he'd always been perceived early on as presenting a bleak or depressing outlook, but he said something similar in that it takes so much energy to put this stuff out and it's so much more complex than that.

WO: Right. If it's fatalistic content, supposedly bleak content, it's being denied by the medium itself. And, the idea behind that is to be encouraging to anybody who shares some of those ideas. Because at the end of the day, sometimes you just feel like God put another anvil on your back and that the best thing to do would be to fall forward and let the anvil crush your ribs— just give in right there.

But as long as there is some sort of harmony going on with another being, if another being is creating some music or conversation, even if it's harmony about this momentary or permanent bleak existence, it can give color and nuance and vitality to something that seems like it would be inherently the opposite.

Like, there is no way you could make darkness fun; but there is. You can. And it doesn't mean you have to give up… like the goth chics don't have to let their roots grow out and get rid of their cheek piercings in order to enjoy themselves. You don't have to change your worldview in order to be energetically engaged with this brief existence.

MJ: I'm interested in what you think about the idea of songs being fables, the idea that a good song should teach you something.

WO: Yeah, that's an ideal that I aspire towards. I have found, increasingly, as I get older, that a lot of the songs that are most important to me are songs that continue to teach me things, sometimes over the course of, God knows, maybe thirty years. Songs that I can enjoy on some level on the first listen at age 15 and then get more into it at age 23 and more into at age 35. And the listening experience is completely different, and I never could have gotten to this different level of listening if I hadn't started with it a long time ago. There are things put in there for your enjoyment and things put in there, ideally, for your edification. If it has legs, then you can one day get to the center of the tootsie pop.

MJ: It's almost like being a philosopher in some ways. That might be too big of a word, but in some of your songs you are searching for wisdom.

WO: Right. Searching for wisdom, which, you know, almost by its definition can only come with time and experience. So searching for ways to endure until that wisdom is possibly showered upon you or revealed through intense polishing.

MJ: I'm wondering if you saw the movie *I'm Not There*[2].

WO: I haven't seen it, no.

MJ: One of the main ideas I got from the film is the work Dylan had to do to change; the work an artist has to do to find the ability to freely try new things. I've read that your Bonnie "Prince" Billy persona was made for that end, originally.

WO: Yeah. It's kind of a parallel existence. In some ways

2 A 2007 biopic on Bob Dylan, directed by Todd Haynes, where six actors play Dylan in an attempt to show his many artistic transformations and/or personas. The most talked-about Dylan roles in the movie were performed by a young African-American man (Marcus Carl Franken) and a woman (Cate Blanchett).

it's a parallel existence and in some ways it's a full on myth world or fable world and in some ways it's also like this alter ego superhero. And in that way it's an amalgam of the different superheroes that I read about when I was a kid.

And when I was a kid, the best comics, if I remember right—because I haven't read comics in a long time— treated the juvenile reader with possibly undue respect and tried to make complicated relationships between the characters in the comic books. And so growing up I could take the concept of having more than one identity, necessarily, because of what you do. I feel like I had some basic education through comic books, and now to have multiple identities.

I'm about to go on tour in a week or so. And most of my vocalization on any given day on a tour will be these songs—not conversation—it will be singing these songs. That can kind of mess with you. Maybe it doesn't with Barry Manilow or Wayne Newton or Glenn Danzig or whoever, but it can mess with your sense of reality.

I think I try to keep one eye on writing the songs in terms of thinking "okay, you know, you are going to live here, you are going to live in these songs, so be careful what you say and be careful how you say it."

There was that movie that wasn't very good with Ben Affleck. I think it was a John Woo movie based on a Phillip K. Dick story called *Paycheck*, where his character knows that he is going to either travel into the future or have his mind erased. So he assembles a set of clues and puts them in a manila envelope and leaves them for himself in the future—so he can reconstruct what happened to him.

There's a little bit of that going on in the songs, knowing that I am going to be giving myself basically into Bonnie's way of being, and that there will be little reminders of what real physical humanity is like, hidden in there, hidden in amongst the songs as I'm singing them. So the re-entry back into the world of physical bleeding will not be as difficult as it has been sometimes in the past.

MJ: So, with the superhero analogy, it's a way of forcing yourself into something greater than you might normally be.

WO: Exactly, forcing it and also allowing it. Oftentimes we feel like we are capable of something, or we know we are capable of something that's better than we would have imagined ourselves capable of. And, we hold ourselves back because there are so many reality checks. The nice thing about music is that once you begin a song or once you begin a set, or once you begin a recording session or a time hidden away in writing, you can sort of shut out the reality checks and know that you're not being something greater than you are capable of being. You're not being something that is greater than you are meant to be. But you are actually giving yourself the chance to not constantly check yourself, inhibit yourself. Because you begin a song, and nobody is going to stop you until you end the song. And you realize, 'okay, that's a free space for me to say and do certain things. And I need to take advantage of all these little two to seven minute capsules of time to say all these things that I've always thought should be said in a way that I've always thought they should be said.' And maybe someone else will be glad that this thing was vocalized in this way.

MJ: Going back to the search for wisdom in songs: I was impressed with the R. Kelly cover on the *Ask Forgiveness* EP[3]. How much searching for wisdom do you do when it comes to R. Kelly-sized music? Because a lot of us might miss it if we are buying a lot of Drag City records.

WO: Yeah. I think a ton. A ton. Some records that sell a lot, sell a lot because of the machinery behind them. Most pop records are sold because of the machinery behind them. And, probably a good percentage of independent records sell because of the current frame of mind, in addition to promo and advertising budgets and things like that.
I was fascinated with the idea of Jimmy Buffet back in the '80s. Looking at the *Rolling Stone* magazine in the '80s, they would always have the top-grossing concert round-up. And, consistently through the '80s, the majority of those shows were The Grateful Dead and Jimmy Buffet. And, neither The Grateful Dead nor Jimmy Buffet had had hit records in years. And neither did you ever see any advertisements for their records, for their shows. These were phenomena that were built by the fan base and maintained by the fan base. And maintained by a respectful relationship between those performers and their audience.

And I tried really hard to understand what it was about Jimmy Buffet that people clung to. People are for the most part smart. The reason they buy bad records that get a lot of push is because they have lives. Most people don't have time to filter out, "should I get this record? or should I get this

3 A Bonnie "Prince" Billy EP released in 2007 that includes cover songs of Bjork, Danzing, Phil Ochs and R. Kelly.

record?" It's more like, "I wanna get a record, I'm gonna get this record." Because they are focusing their energy and their intelligence and their sensitivity on things more important to them than music at that time. But knowing that over the years, masses of people kept returning to Grateful Dead and Jimmy Buffet, I kept thinking there's got to be something there. And there's got to be something there whether or not I find it. There is something there because I'm not going to discredit the devotion of these hundreds of thousands of people. Because if I do that, then I'm dooming myself to complete alienation from society. If I think they are all idiots, then I've screwed myself.

MJ: I'm interested in the theme of family in *Lie Down in the Light*, and I'm curious how you came to think about that, and how that theme works for you in the new album.

WO: I've been fortunate in that something that has been strong and stable in my existence has been my family, and even my extended family to cousins and aunts and uncles and my grandparents and such.... I'm trying to run through my brain music that is family related.

MJ: The Carter Family?

WO: They were a family that played, but I don't know if they sang that much about it. And then there is the country music tradition of singing about the mother. There seems to be a current trend in modern country music to sing about a newborn child or about the daughter leaving the house at a certain age and moving on and becoming an adult. In books and movies, they seem to address more complex family relations, talking about brothers or cousins or grandparents more deeply. And those things have always resonated with me.

There's a writer named Robert Johnson — he has no relation to the musician. In his autobiography, I think it's called *Balancing Heaven and Earth*, he describes growing up without much of a family structure. Then as an adult he decided, "Because I wasn't given a family by birth doesn't mean I can't have one." So he began to nominally create his family and say, "This person is my grandfather, this person is my uncle, this person is my brother," with the idea being that these people, your family, are the unconditional ones. The ones that even when they do wrong, that's when the rules go out the window. That's when you embrace that person even if that person has done what you might not accept in a friend or in a colleague. Someone you continue to support and ideally, be supported by.

I've also been fortunate in my life to be part of a community of people that more or less, we consider each other like cousins, if not brothers and sisters, to the point where I am Uncle Will to a lot of kids that I'm not physically related to. But it's a natural feeling, you know, it feels great. Because when everything else falls apart, those relationships will be there, that they will stand tests of endurance that other relationships will not.

By extension, I feel—of course it can't be as complex, it can't be as deep-rooted, ultimately it can't be as strong in many ways—there is a musical community of players, writers, performers, and especially *listeners*, because I'm sure that I am more of a listener, proportionately, timewise, in my life. I'm more of an audience member than anything else. And I hold a great kinship with people who are avid listeners, who pay attention, who like music that makes them feel good, that illuminates negative feelings, without forcing their hand to take negative action in support of those negative feelings. People who are open and avid and energetic about their relationship to music.

Just Kibbe

Dead Cow Trampoline

Imagine the death of pride—not always a good thing.
Imagine death is a trampoline. Imagine death is not
shaped like a Holstein cow. Imagine the belly, swollen
with games and laughter. Imagine the cow spotted.
The cow is spotted. It is that kind of cow
and three days dead—long enough for its intestines to fill
with methane gas and rise heavenward, long enough
for trinity to grow bored, long enough to discover a bounce
factor equal to the elegant arch of swollen cow-belly.

Don't jump too hard, imagine too keenly or fly too high.
The future scares your mother, catching sight of you
out the kitchen window, yelling "Stop jumping on the dead cow
before someone gets hurt." I listened,
forgot to be careful and earned a nifty scar.

J Michael Wahlgren

*Iron Out

This was a secret operation./ My clientele plummeted like
a stock market./ I unfolded the mess, the heave./ I was a
spy / of subtle seams & wet money in pockets./ I reeled
in the laundry line—/ I filed the pile alphabetically:/ The
powder screaming, burn me, burn me./ Flares wanting to
be converted to gas./ I plugged the iron in. / I was similar
to a lexicon, then,/ melting soft origami,/ The shifting of/
an avalanche of ice, I, / could cross with the sky./ The
smell inserted itself without/ the powder. The gas— / this
burning; the paper into life. / This was my astronautical
dream as a youth:/ my sweet tooth.

Revolutionary Women
OF THE IRONING BOARD

Non-Fiction by Leslie Patterson

Edgar Degas created almost thirty works depicting laundresses, but when I see his 1884 painting *Ironing Women* at the Orsay Museum, I know it is my favorite. In the painting, the artist shows two women standing behind a large table or counter. The woman on the right presses hard on her iron with both hands. She seems to be standing on her toes in order to put her whole weight behind her work. Her head is bent in concentration so that her face is entirely obscured by a luxurious knot of red hair. With her sleeves rolled up to expose her meaty arms, she gives the sea green garment she is ironing a walloping. In contrast, the woman on the left side of the canvas is idle. She is yawning with her mouth uncovered, unabashedly exposing her double chin. One of her hands is raised beside her head in a theatrical stretch. Her other hand clasps a bottle of wine. The woman's lassitude suggests that she's polished off a good bit of the bottle already.

I like these big broads of the ironing board, one at work, the other at rest. For me, the two postures of the women in the picture say something about the nature of their task. For although in Degas's era, ironing was hard, heavy work, today, for me, it is one of those marvelous activities where the body is busy but the mind is free. When I am ironing, it is as if I am two women, twice what I usually am.

I don't think that I am alone in this feeling. Recently, when I asked a group of friends their opinions about ironing, most of them confessed a little guiltily to liking the chore. Their responses made me wonder for the first time in my life how my mother felt about ironing.

The ironing board was a constant presence in my childhood: in the picture of my mother that I carry in my mind, she is always standing behind a padded board with a basket of drifted laundry at her feet. And yet, despite these associations, I did not learn to iron from my mother. Rather, it was my paternal grandmother, surprised at my teenage incompetence, who taught me how to press a dress shirt in perfect order and at breakneck speed: underside of collar, inside of collar, yoke, sleeves, placket, and the rest. My mother, with her overflowing basket, never called me in to take my place in the ranks of the ironing women.

I always assumed that she did not enlist me for the same reason that she did not teach me to cook. I assumed ironing was a task that she considered to be onerous drudgery, something that she hoped would not be an essential part of her daughters's more affluent and intellectual lives. She might stand behind the padded board with a can of spray starch at her elbow and a steaming iron in her hand, its cord enclosed in a little argyle sleeve, but in her dreams, my sister and I would not.

But now I wonder if I could be mistaken in attributing this motivation to my mother. Did she too secretly enjoy ironing?

When she ironed my father's Air Force uniforms and the white cotton shirts that I perversely began wearing in high school when everyone else was wearing black, my mother watched television. It was the only time she allowed herself this indulgence. Once a week, on Sunday at eight o'clock, she would flip on the set and watch *Masterpiece Theatre*. And as she watched Thérèse Raquin murder her husband in a lake or Miss Elizabeth Bennett reconcile herself to love with Mr. Darcy, the iron would sputter and spit its way across acres of fabric. By the time Alistair Cooke said goodnight, hangers lined the side of her ironing board and clogged the door knobs of our rec room. I would take my snowy items upstairs to the brassy blasts of the show's classical theme song.

I always found this combination of the high, *Masterpiece Theatre*, and the low, ironing, in my mother's life curious.

But looking back, every bit of her life has contained these contradictions. She is a British woman with a posh accent, who immigrated to California with her family when she was fourteen. The accent is a relic of the exclusive schools she attended as a scholarship student. She is one of the most well-read and intelligent people I've ever known, and yet her formal education went no further than high school. She is a pacifist with a belief in the kinds of social welfare programs usually only found in Europe, and yet she is married to an enlisted man, a lifer in the U.S. military. She is a woman who professes not to like children but is always the first one in the neighborhood to be pressed into babysitting or leading a Girl Scout troop. She is absolutely trustworthy yet dreamy. She is patient and calm, except for one day a year when someone, usually my older sister, pushes her too far, and then, she throws things. So, perhaps, on those nights I remember that seem so odd, my mother felt most normal. When she was ironing and watching a costume drama, she was able to fully be the two-sided being that she really is.

When I was eighteen and first attended university, so much was unfamiliar: girls donned miraculous new dresses every night as they vied to get into sororities, tan kids talked of summers in Bulgaria and Greece, and a bespectacled art history teacher described having a champagne picnic on the paw of the Sphinx. All this made me desperate for anything that reminded me of my old life. Flipping through a literature textbook, I almost cried when I saw a short story titled *I Stand Here Ironing*.

From Tillie Olsen's first line, "I stand here ironing, and what you ask me moves tormented back and forth with the iron," I was riveted. The story was about mothers and daughters and all the daily, exhausting, soul-killing, maintenance tasks of a hard-working life. Olsen detailed the kind of life where illness provided the only thing like a vacation and the task of ironing was welcome because it offered the luxury of time to think. It was not my life, thank God, that the story described, but it held a bit of my mother's life in it. The story was like a great aunt, immediately recognizable if one generation removed.

The first time I remember seeing my mother cry, she was at an ironing board. I must have been about four. Our family had just moved to Texas. There, my father, fresh from his year in Vietnam, spent his days working on Randolph Brooks Air Force Base and his nights selling appliances at Montgomery Ward. My mother babysat and kept frantic notes on every penny we spent in a little green account book. One night, an ambulance took my father away. My mother set up her ironing board and sobbed. I can't really say what time it was when I woke and crept out of bed to see her crying. At that age, every hour beyond 9 p.m. had the feeling of being very strange and very late. So that I'm sure it only seemed to me as if my mother was wetting every piece of clothing in the house with her tears before she ironed the wet drops out. But I know I did not mistake the fear that my mother felt. She was worried about my father and worried that one serious illness could cause us to slip into the terrifying financial mess of Tillie Olsen's characters.

Now, I too iron and clean when confronted with trouble. It is another way of being two women—the one who is forced to endure the disorder and wrinkly chaos of life and the one who frantically tries to iron it out and put the world back together again.

It's fitting that Olsen, a labor leader, should have written a famous story about ironing: laundresses have played a substantial role in the labor movement. In New York, in 1864, the first female union in the country, the Collar Laundry Union, was created by a woman named Kate Mullaney, and in 1881, the Atlanta Washerwoman's Strike struck a blow for black laundresses and sent ripples of revolution through the entire black working community. Recently, critics have even suggested that all those French nineteenth century paintings of laundresses and ironing women were inspired by the role laundresses played in establishing worker's rights. In France, where laundry services were considered so essential that they were often written into workers' contracts, laundresses were some of the first laborers to succeed in achieving better working hours and wages through strikes and collective bargaining. These women with arms made ropey and strong from beating the dirt out of fabrics and lifting heavy loads, were formidable figures, far better paid than any other female laborers and feared for the cohesiveness of their largely female workplaces.

By the time I was ten, my mother worked full-time in a windowless factory for a mail order company. The company, which had a ridiculously patrician name, produced cheap and relentlessly ugly merchandise for budget-minded consumers. My sister and I consistently called the place a "sweatshop" as if we expected a *Norma Rae* style strike to break out at any minute. When it didn't, we made our mother's work there the butt of jokes.

At the company, my mother worked on a machine that pressed folds into gaudy greeting cards. Her hours would spike in the days leading up to Christmas when last minute shoppers would scramble to send a red and gold card of a charmless sleigh or a maniacal elf to their relatives and friends. At that time of the year, my mother worked from five in the morning until four in the afternoon. To watch her work these eleven-hour days and then come home to deal with the jovial obligations of our increasingly middle class holiday season came to seem like going outside to watch a hurricane: you knew you were going to get wet and windblown but nonetheless it was hard not to be transfixed by the disaster.

One night, when my sister was seventeen and I was fifteen, my mother had set the ironing board up in the kitchen as she cooked dinner. She ran back and forth between cutting vegetables and ironing a frothy pink dress that my sister was going to wear to a dance that night. I did my homework hunt-and-peck-style at a typewriter on the kitchen table. My sister talked on the phone. My mother's face flushed angrily like the metal on a hot kettle, and snow fell placidly outside.

When my sister got off the phone, she told my mother that she could stop ironing. The dance had been canceled; some kid had gotten himself killed driving on the snowy roads. "I hope you're happy now," my sister said as if my mother had planned the weather just to thwart her.

My mother looked up from her chopping block and said "you ungrateful brat." With her right hand she began slapping my sister's face while in her left hand she still held her kitchen knife. Her slaps sent my sister closer and closer to the ironing board, until my mother at last came to herself. In frustration, she grabbed the can of spray starch sitting on the ironing board and threw it across the room where it ricocheted from the stove to the typewriter, forever ruining the carriage.

And I suppose it's this incident that stops me from asking my mother about her feelings concerning ironing. Perhaps my thought that ironing allows me to be two women is a strictly generational concept, a nostalgic idea bred by a life of relative leisure. For me, ironing will always be more of a pastime than a chore. After all, I have never spent a day lifting a heavy iron from a sweating stove nor have I hauled great baskets of fresh linen on my arms through the streets of Paris. Instead, in that beautiful city, I visit a museum and see two women standing at Degas' ironing board, one representing the hardworking women of the past and the other a premonition of our present leisure. It is a lovely sight, and I am grateful. In a nearby bistro, I lift a bottle to my mother and all the revolutionary women of the ironing board.

sept 29.   elastic cycle. i used to be a
go-overer and now am a come-overer. waiting
for one who would rou~~d~~t me from my slumber
home. sadness, which i though was an inward
domain, has seeped into the surroundings
again. she floats effortless on the surface
of water, a no-time there with her. she dan
ces holographically before you, ever emerging,
ever arriving at a dissolution of the barrier
between,that had only seemed to be there. i
move out of the sadness, through the other-por
tal to the higher self, a totemic ritual relat
ion to the divine unity, goddess and god. the
container of the self is ~~visceu~~ porous and the
viscous medium of identity seethes from fissures
and holes in the vessel. identity as a process
of identification with, an extension into nove
lty with another. the special magic that attend
ds to that moment, the discovery of composition
fleeting in the emergent perpetual creation.
a feather the size of my fingernail lands stick
ing to the back og my hand. it clings to the
surface of hand, lifted and flipped by the wind
and gusts of breath from her lips, pursed to
blow a challenge to the precarious moment. he
who travels by air must migrate with the seaso
nal procession, lifted more by wind than will,
the ideogram, eye above person, active and rec
eptive sight. i will go to meet the goddess
of wands with my vessel overflowing. water-
body extending amoeboid psuedopods out towards
a protean embrace. she will change her form
each element, each animal, each object taken
into the embrace until the ~~b~~ wall develops
cracks and the contents of that container too
begin to seep out into the surrounding sea of
uncertainty, ~~virus-ber~~ the tension that holds
memory that hides, desire that seeks.

by Mark DeRespinis

Jessy Randall

Setting the Type

At last, my crush
on the letters of the alphabet
gets physical.

I reach for the _e_, the _t_, the _f_
each in its own little compartment
the ink staining my fingers.

The _w_ is more beautiful than I
ever imagined.
The capital _H_ deserves its own sonnet.

But I am careless.
I drop them all.

They splay out from my hands,
ring as they hit the floor.

I am lost without them.

4891 – How Jesus was Right and George Orwell Got It Backwards.

START
AVIN

newspaper
to se...

Losing your job doesn...
to mean losing your M...

Fiction by Matthew Britt

Jesus is on CNN saying that if you can hear him right now, if you're listening, then you're not going to Heaven. He says this in English, and after the translator has her turn, the people who waited for days and days outside King Solomon's Temple to see Jesus give the same sound as if they had been gut checked by Goliath.

But on CNN Jesus' face is blacked out because of a copyright lawsuit filed by Fig Marketing Agency. These are the same people that bought up all the website addresses before the Dot.Com bust. These are the same people who buy up the most likely drug names when a drug company receives funding for research. So they bought the rights to all images and likenesses of Jesus, in case he were to ever return.

Fig Marketing Agency tried to copyright the letter E, but after appealing all the way to the Supreme Court the letter E, along with all letters, remained public domain.

On the 767 direct from JFK to Jerusalem watching T.V. used to be included in the flight, but with rising gas prices, if I want to continue watching Jesus on CNN, it's going to cost me another dollar for the next half hour. Of course I slide my credit card because I'm taking notes on everything Jesus is saying. For the last week I haven't turned off CNN. They have the best religious team on TV, they say, and I'm playing catch-up to try and figure out what all of this means. I thought I knew, like a lot of people thought they knew, but if this really is Jesus, which it just might be, then what we thought we knew was wrong.

One week ago I was sitting in my Bloomington, Indiana, apartment eating Cheetos. What I used to do for a living is I used to be the movie critic for the *Herald Times*, but as newspapers die off to the internet, the first people to get fired from newspapers are movie critics. For much, much less than what the paper used to pay me, which wasn't much, they now buy nationally syndicated articles from freelance writers. So, for now at least, I don't know what to do with my life besides eat Cheetos in my dark apartment and watch the American Film Institute's top 100 movies of all time while collecting unemployment.

I could start a blog online and continue to critique movies, for free.

Or I could go look for another job. But no one is hiring journalists.

I saw that the video store was hiring, but unemployment pays a little better than minimum wage.

So, I was eating Cheetos watching *The Best Years of Our Lives* and Googling my high school girlfriend that I haven't seen or heard from in over a decade. She wasn't on Google images. No MySpace page. She's not on Facebook. I was checking my email so that I could delete the messages from the Canadian Online Pharmacy that I keep marking as Junk, but somehow keep getting into my inbox. Amazon has special deals for me, and eBay wants me to look at all the items I'm watching in my eBay account, but that I won't bid on or buy. It's just a list of things I want to buy someday when I'm not on unemployment.

And there was an email from Jesus.

Of course I think this is junk mail from a Mexican pharmacy, but the message title is "Interview", so I open the message. It says that in the mail tomorrow will be a plane ticket to Jerusalem, where I will have a one on one interview with Jesus himself. He's come back because he has a message that I'm going to help him deliver to the world, and I should turn on CNN in twenty minutes.

Since then, for the last week, CNN has had their religious team, the best religious team on TV, debating what all of this could mean. Jesus gave one short interview, where he said, with his face blacked out, that he would give a speech from the Temple of King Solomon, and then he would give a one-on-one interview with one handpicked reporter. Then he walked around a Jerusalem neighborhood turning water into wine, making the lame walk, and giving sight to the blind.

On CNN, you couldn't see his face, but Jesus said, "Some of my greatest hits so you'll know I am who I say I am."

The next day a plane ticket came in the mail. It wasn't first class or anything, I guess the tightening economy has affected Jesus too, although he's not really a first class kind of guy.

But let me back up a little bit further than Cheetos and unemployment. A few years ago, beyond reviewing movies, I had a column in a small Christian magazine: I was the resident Atheist. Whether people were questioning their faith or just didn't understand how someone couldn't believe in God, they could write me, and I'd answer their questions. Kind of an Atheist Ann Landers.

Even after I answered the question the first time, and reprinted the original article three times, the question I received most was, "If you don't believe in Heaven and Hell, why don't you go out and kill a lot of people?"

Some people really believe that if you're not afraid of God, then you're not afraid of anything.

Before that I grew up in a religious house where we read the Bible every night. We went to Sunday meeting, and Wednesday night Bible study. We didn't have a T.V. because T.V. distracted from doing the work of God. We weren't Amish. We drove cars and went to public school, but we were kind of weird.

And I went to college where I watched lots and lots of movies, studied journalism, and became an Atheist.

Some people would say that was just me rebelling. Like my parents would say this.

But here I am on my way to meet Jesus, watching Jesus on T.V, and asking the flight attendant for another whiskey and coke.

This is one of those, "If you could have dinner with anyone dead or living, who would it be?" moments.

On the T.V. Jesus is saying that if you can hear him, if you're listening, then you're not going to Heaven. He's saying that Revelations happened two thousand years ago. He's saying everyone left here, we were the meek he was talking about, and we've inherited the Earth.

"I'm not here to bring Salvation," Jesus says.

"All I'm going to do is try to save you from yourselves," Jesus says.

"The chosen ones have already gone to Heaven," Jesus says.

Clearly I'm going to have to ask him what he means by this. Because if I'm hearing him right, what he's saying is that none of us is going anywhere.

I'm adding this to my list of questions that I've been working on for the last week. You know, the basics, like: Did Judas betray you? Do you know how to read and write? What's your favorite movie? Have you had a chance to listen to The Beatles White Album?

And yes, I know there was a reason I did movie reviews.

The flight attendant brings me the whiskey and coke, and these drinks used to be free on oceanic flights, but every whiskey and coke costs me another five dollars. And it's five dollars even, so I don't know if tax is included, or since we're over the middle of the Atlantic, if taxes don't apply.

I've got another question to ask Jesus, now that I'm thinking of it. He's all big into give unto Caesar what's Caesar's and all of that great tax advice, but why is it that you're charged sales tax when you rent a movie? You're not buying the movie, so there's no sale of merchandise. The city and county and state are all taking money from every video rental transaction. And then when the video store sells the video, when they put it in their Hot Deals box, they charge sales tax on it again.

I mean, Jesus used to be about injustice, right?

And yes, I know, just because you get to have dinner with any person dead or alive doesn't mean that YOU will have something interesting to say.

On T.V. Jesus is saying that we have painted ourselves into a corner.

"God isn't watching over you," he says. "There is no big brother. George Orwell had it backwards: you've all become so consumed with all the distractions that the distractions are what control you.

"You've become so consumed with the darnel weeds that you're also pulling out the wheat," he says.

"More of my greatest hits: Matthew thirteen twenty four," he says.

"Trying to escape from the trap is just another trap. You have to let the weeds grow if you want to cultivate the wheat," he says.

There weren't any hotel accommodations with the plane ticket, and with all those whiskey and cokes, and all of that CNN coverage on the plane, unemployment isn't going to do much better than The Petra Hostel. The cab driver, who I know spoke perfectly good English, tried to charge me a flat rate to the hostel. I told him to start the meter, because in my *Lonely Planet: Jerusalem*, well, not mine, but in the Bloomington Indiana's public library copy of *Lonely Planet: Jerusalem* it says that this flat rate scam is commonly pulled on tourists.

And here's the other thing, when I think of Jerusalem I picture the Jews in the desert for forty years. If they find a tree in the desert, they're going to call it the holy land and set up camp. And with all this "conflict", as they call it on CNN, I picture Detroit. But not Detroit on the frozen tundra of Michigan, but I picture Detroit in the middle of the Arizona desert: after World War III.

But the airport, let's see if I can say this right, the Ben Gurion International is way cleaner than Detroit Metro, but judging by the cabby's meter, it's not even half as close as Detroit Metro, and Detroit Metro is in the middle of nowhere. But right now this place is packed with every Jesus freak, historian, preacher, and, let's not forget, the media. But I guess I'm part of the media, so I'll keep it to myself and be glad that I even got a bunk in the hostel.

The rest of the city, just from the back of the taxi, and from the views at the hostel, this city is amazing. Like I said, this was not on my top-ten list of places to go on vacation. Jerusalem would have been down there with Baltimore, Newark, New Jersey, and Stockton, California, but this place has a few thousand years of culture on New York City, and it shows. Picture Manhattan in the middle of the Roman ruins.

And more people speak English than in Stockton.

Walking around Old City, as Lonely Planet calls it, this is Jesus' old stomping grounds. And by stomping grounds, I mean this is where he flipped out on the vendors and overturned the marketplace. On my notepad I write, "Could you imagine this is what Jerusalem would look like two thousand years later?" Right now, everything is a question. Have you had McDonald's? Do you eat? Do they have food in heaven?

You know, all the important stuff.

My flight home leaves tomorrow night, so this is all the time I get to walk around the holy land. I mean, if you're going to interview Jesus, which should take a few hours, and you're going to eat and sleep, exactly how long should you spend at the Wailing Wall before moving on to the Al-Aqsa Mosque, the place where Mohammad ascended to heaven.

Not that this trip is about Mohammad.

But if you could sit in the same spot as Buddha under the tree of knowledge, wouldn't you do it?

Jesus wants to meet me at The King David Hotel, in his room. Judging by the structure, Jesus is not on the same budget I am. But I'm sure King David being Jesus' great great great great great grandpa, or however many greats it is, I'm sure King David doesn't mind giving Jesus the Holy Suite for a few nights. But as I'm trying to get in, Security pushes me into the crowd and says, "Get back."

And John Lennon might have been wrong because, judging by this crowd, The Beatles were not more popular than Jesus.

"I'm here to see Jesus," I say.

"You and everyone else," Security says. Actually, he laughs.

"No, I'm here to interview him. He invited me," I say.

"We've got a freak out here," Security says into the CB radio attached to his shoulder as he looks me up and down. And then he moves to the side and says, "Go."

In the lobby there's a whole team of security guards who pat me down and metal wand me.

In the elevator it was me in the middle of nine security guards.

Up in Jesus' room, or master suite, whatever, there are all these people walking around in white robes. The security guys stop at the door, and one of the robed guys inside tells me to have a seat in a big, comfy, leather chair. He asks me if I want some wine, and I say, "Do you have any whiskey?"

"Of course. On the rocks?" he asks.

"Oh please," I say. "With an inch of water."

Looking around the room, this is not the picture The New Testament paints of Jesus. All of these other guys go sit around a big conference table, and the one brings me back the whiskey. "Thanks," I say.

"Of course," the guy says and then sits down on the chair across from me. "Did you have a good flight?" he asks.

"It was alright," I say taking a drink from the glass. "But I guess you don't complain about airplane food when you're going to meet Jesus," I say. I know this isn't funny, but I've never been great at these nervous moments. Who wants to talk about how those free peanut bags are feeling a little lighter now-a-days when history is in the making?

"Oh, I'm sorry," the guy says extending his hand, "I'm Jesus. I keep forgetting about that copyright lawsuit. Not exactly what you were expecting?" he says.

"I thought you'd be taller," I say.

And you don't have to tell me, I know, not my shining moment.

"Do you have a tape recorder?" Jesus asks.

"Uhm, yeah," I say reaching for my bag.

"Good," Jesus says. "There's something I need to tell everyone, and I want to make sure that you understand me clearly."

By the way, Jesus is even better looking than all of those Renaissance paintings portray. Picture Brad Pitt in *Legends of the Fall*, but shorter, and add a bit of Gandhi, but not the real Gandhi, but Ben Kingsley, the guy that played Gandhi in the movie.

All great leaders are good looking, why would Jesus be any different?

"Well, don't you want me to ask you questions?" I ask.

"No, I just want you to listen, and then if you have questions about what I'm saying, you can ask."

"Well, can I at least ask why you picked me?"

Jesus takes a deep breath looking away from me, and says, "Sure.

"I saw you on public television debating a preacher.

You were saying that Christianity wasn't marketing itself very well, and that Evolution was a bad place for Christianity to challenge Science. You were well thought out and made great points."

"So, wait," I say, "you watch television?"

"It's all electromagnetic waves," Jesus says. "Heaven is a real place. Now listen."

Behind Jesus, at the table, I'm counting heads, and there are eleven people. Half of them have their backs to me, and I can't see if one of them is Mary Magdalene.

"Humanity is going to die off if you don't listen," Jesus says. "God may have already come and gone, but I still have a soft spot for the meek, and Climate Change is real. But you've got it all wrong."

Behind Jesus one of the guys says to the others at the table, "That's right, it's all the roll of the dice."

"Look," Jesus says, "Climate Change isn't caused by carbon dioxide. The scientists haven't figured it out yet. If you want to save yourselves, if you want to have a planet left to inherit, a place for your children's children to thrive and play, you need to understand the problem so you can understand the solution."

Behind Jesus one of the guys says, "That's right: it's all based on the Chance card."

"Carbon dioxide isn't the problem. The problem is sound waves. There is too much noise on this planet. All of the sound waves are bouncing around against each other which causes friction. Friction causes heat. Haven't you ever noticed that temperatures are higher around population centers?"

Behind Jesus one of the guys says, but this is clearly a woman's voice, she says, "I'm going to win with nothing more than Baltic Avenue."

"You don't need to drive fuel efficient cars to cut down on air pollution; you need to ride bicycles to cut down on noise pollution," Jesus says. "With more people on the planet you're creating more noise. There are seven billion people talking and listening to the radio and buying battery operated toys for their screaming babies. You all have vacuum cleaners and power tools and lawn mowers. Not to mention airplanes, industrial production, and Dr. Phil. If you want to save yourselves, if you really care about the human race, you all need to shut up."

Kathleen Willard

Dachau

In my garden, the small fists of ferns uncurl.
This day marks the anniversary of the liberation of Dachau.
Forty thousand survivors crossed the fence to freedom.

And I recall my mother, a decade after
armistice, visiting the camp, a young officer's wife.
She will always remember
the map tracing the origins of the dead.

Not just the Jews, but someone from Mongolia
and an entire tribe of Polish gypsies. None of us are safe.
The bowed heads of my shooting stars parachute open.

The neighbors denied they lived next door to a slaughterhouse.
They never saw the black smoke from the brick ovens
or acknowledged the smell.

Forty thousand is half the size of my town. I imagine
the volley of rifle shots
and round the clock digging of mass graves,
the mountains of abandoned

shoes and the monstrous tangle of shorn hair--
all of this the residents of Dachau hope to wish away.
    Abracadabra, followed by a grammatically incorrect tract
declaring

the whole thing a hoax just like landing
on the moon. The heirloom forsythia, my husband considers
  too weedy, waves its yellow arms.

MONGOLIA!

MONGOLIA!

Evolution of an Ancient World

Non-Fiction & Photography by Julie Larson

Deep in the Gorkhi-Terelj National Park in central Mongolia, a 70-year-old man proudly pointed to a black dot on his index finger, eager to tell me its significance: he had voted in the national election. It was June 29, 2008, near the heart of Mongolia. The man sold jewelry to travelers from a tiny kiosk located near the base of a rock formation called Turtle Rock. After 70 years, I could only imagine the remarkable changes this man has seen in his homeland.

The Mongolian people have lived through a tumultuous history—from the Huns and Turks, to the great Genghis Khan, or Chinggis Khaan as they call him. In more recent times, the Mongolians have contended with Chinese and Soviet rule. In 1990, with the deterioration of Soviet communist rule, Mongolia underwent a democratic revolution. The revolution resulted in the formation of a multi-party parliamentary government, the creation of a constitution in 1992, and the introduction of a free press.

Mongolia's first free election in 1990 ushered in the Mongolian People's Revolutionary Party (MPRP), the former communist party. The first noncommunist government was elected in 1996, but the MPRP regained power again in the 2000 elections.

The June 2008 legislative election results awarded the MPRP a majority of parliamentary seats. The opposing Democratic Party, claiming a fraudulent vote tally, publicly challenged the election results. The Democratic Party's claims turned a peaceful protest in front of the MPRP headquarters on July 1, 2008, into a deadly riot. While Mongolia has endured political unrest for years, this use of violence was quite uncommon.

The MPRP headquarters was gutted by a fire set by protestors hurling bottles of alcohol through the windows of the building. Police, suited in full riot gear, attempted to control the riot by firing rubber bullets and tear gas into the crowd and using their batons when in close range. As vehicles were set ablaze nearby, the MPRP headquarters was looted and the fire spread to the nearby Mongolian Modern Art Gallery and the performing arts auditorium. Arson was also reported at the headquarters of three Mongolian newspapers: *Hummuussiin Amidral, Humuus* and *Unuudriin Mongol.* The violence left five people dead and a reported 710 people were detained. President Enkhbayar declared a state of emergency and Mongolian tanks rolled through the capital city.

"As part of the declaration [the president] ordered all television stations off the air except Mongolian National Broadcasting (MNB), which is ostensibly a public station, not a state-run station," said Brian White, the resident director of the American Center for Mongolian Studies in Ulaanbaatar. "This continued until the declaration expired 4 days later, and then all other stations came back on the air."

The Mongolian people were particularly interested in the 2008 election because it effectively decided who controls the development of Mongolia's wealth of natural resources. Mongolia's countryside is rich in mineral resources, especially copper. The extraction of minerals is expected to generate significant wealth. Whoever controls these national resources is projected to amass considerable power and riches. The Democratic Party believes that corporations should be given the right to develop the mineral deposits, while the MPRP intends to maintain government control of the resources. There is a considerable amount of money at stake for the people of Mongolia and the MPRP as worldwide demand for copper increased prices to unprecedented levels.

Mongolia's copper mining epicenter, Erdenet, is located north of the nation's capital. The city's architecture and local cuisine is reminiscent of the Soviet communist past, with square buildings, vodka, and Borsch. To learn more about how Mongolia's nomadic herding population views the country's transition to democracy and freedom of the press, I visited a tourist ger camp, just northwest of Erdenet.

Nestled into the rolling green hills, the camp is established near a nomadic herding family who lives one quarter of the year in the valley. The patriarch of the family is named Tumen Nasan. An older gentleman, Nasan, has raised livestock his entire life, mostly during communist rule. Under the Soviet communist rule, Nasan said he was only allowed to own "16 livestock, including 12 sheep or goats, two horses, and two cows." He earned a living by herding the government-owned animals. Since 1990, livestock has been privatized, and Nasan now owns over 1,000 head of livestock—100 horses and 900 sheep and goats—for which he has obtained the title of "Myangat Malchin," or "greatest herder." While the number of livestock and lavishness of his horse saddles can be used to gauge Nasan's wealth in the nomadic community, he earns most of his income from raising prize-winning racehorses. Nasan believes that he and his family have benefited greatly from Mongolia's transition to a free market, but he is apprehensive about the nation's politics.

When asked what he thought of the riots in Ulaanbaatar, Nasan suggested that the individuals who took part in the rioting were young adults who had been abandoned and forced to live on the streets of the capital city when the Soviets pulled out of Mongolia in 1990. He believes these youth grew up without a formal education, and they consequently blame the former communist party (MPRP) for their plight. Nasan had watched coverage of the riots in Ulaanbaatar through satellite television.

Through Mongolia's transition to democracy, the Mongolian Constitution has served as a guide for freedom of the press and government transparency, but these

practices have not been effectively enforced. While the Mongolian Constitution promises the right of the people to obtain information and distribute it freely, journalists's experiences have illuminated a severe lack of effective law enforcement. The Freedom House organization's rating of Mongolia's freedom of the press has been declining since the nation's democratic revolution. The Freedom House originally rated the nation's media as "free" in 1994 through 2002, but has rated the country as "partially free" since 2002. Censorship laws enacted to reduce access to government information are greatly jeopardizing the freedom of the press in Mongolia, and consequently the stability of the democracy. This censorship ranges from harassment and threats of physical harm, to tax audits and legal action (mainly slander and libel lawsuits).

The freedom of Mongolia's press remains in a precarious position. During Soviet communist rule, the Mongolian media was closely regulated, producing state-run newspapers and local government radio and television programming. Since the late 1990s, Mongolia's media landscape has expanded dramatically, with the development of an estimated 340 media outlets and the introduction of Internet-based news. Media development has progressed substantially within the nation of 2.9 million people, but the freedom of the press remains in jeopardy. Mongolia is currently facing two major challenges in the pursuit of an independent, ethical media: government censorship and a lack of professional ethical standards.

An editor at the *UB Post*, an English language weekly paper in Ulaanbaatar described how the newspaper industry in Mongolia generally operates. He requested that his name not be used. According to the editor, many heads of newspapers have familial ties with the mine owners and heads of state. These associations then dictate what news the paper publishes about Mongolia's lucrative mining industry and the government. Additionally, he has found that practicing journalists receive very little education in their profession, and are not held to strict standards of ethical journalism.

In 2007, UNESCO conducted an analysis of Mongolia's media ethics. According to the report, "Fifteen years since Mongolia's move to democracy, there is still little to no understanding of how to manage and grow an independent and balanced media outlet that exists for the sake of providing free and independent information or for the sake of being a business in itself, without having to depend on political and/or business support."

The report documented numerous infractions against Mongolian journalists who published investigative reports on government and mining actions. "In June, 2006, [a female journalist] reported on the fate of privatization vouchers for 9,000 employees of the Erdenet mining industry. After the television program, unknown people threatened [the journalist] over the phone. The director of the Erdenet brokerage company, which held the vouchers, also warned the journalist, 'It is a very complicated issue, you could be killed.' In July, 2006 she was beaten by unidentified perpetrators, and was hospitalized for treatment."

The complex transition from communism to democracy has also divided the people of Mongolia from one uniform social class into an upper and a lower class. While visiting the steppe of the Gobi Desert, I asked a young Mongol, Erkhembaatar Tseenyambuu, about his perception of how the country and the people have changed since the fall of communism. Tseenyambuu's family owns a tourist camp near Dalanzadgad in the southern part of the country. The camp is comprised of a main dining facility, a shower building, and a cluster of gers (traditional Mongolian round houses, also called yurts).

Although Tseenyambuu was born in 1985 and does

not remember everyday life under Soviet communist rule, he has learned a great deal through his parents' experiences. Personally, he has "seen much change in recent years, with the gap between the rich and the poor widening." But Tseenyambuu believes his family is doing well. He has studied abroad in Japan and plans to continue his education of the Japanese culture. With democratic rule, he said, "students can study wherever they want to. The internet is also beneficial—it's how we get our news [in the Gobi]." In the future, Tseenyambuu would like to maintain the family tourism business, but for now, he is focused on his formal education.

The transition from a uniform social class into an upper and lower class is evident throughout Mongolia's populous capital city and the sparsely populated countryside. My translator Namuun Batnavch explained, "before 1990 everyone was of the same social class—they owned nothing. In 1990, the privatization of factories and properties, and start of trade with China established large companies and corporations. When the state-owned factories were privatized, they distributed stock options to the people on red and blue paper. They gave everyone the stock options, but most people didn't know how to trade them and just kept them at home." This rapid transition into a free market economy with democratic ideals posed opportunities for many Mongolians, but was detrimental for those who were unable to adapt. "Most people didn't know how to survive in a democratic country," said Batnavch. "Smart people picked up the opportunity, but those who did not recognize the market or realize the period went into a lower social class."

Driven by a simultaneous fusion of nationalism, tradition, modernization, and globalization, Mongolia is undergoing a tremendous evolution—unparalleled anywhere else in the world today. With corrupted global mining interests and the challenge of integrating the nomadic herding population's needs with the needs of those who reside in the cities, Mongolia has reached a pivotal developmental crossroads. It is a land of ancient history where the winds of the steppes whisper history and the chatter of satellite television fills a ger. Whether desired or not, Mongolia is in the vortex of change that will shape the future of a free press and the future of this fragile democracy.

Felicia Zamora

The Beach on June 11, 2008

Something about an ocean
brittles bones. Salt churns
over into salt
tight and compact
nooks in nooks
spawning
in and on and through
water to skin, between toes,
in nostrils, to the heart.

Pump beats
breaking waves
rhythms and eardrums.
Land of stone
breasts heave
coral, seaweed, crab-
shells, places to hide
our visions of our eyes
reflected.

Her body – lamina,
leaving and washing
pebbles to gravel to soft grained white.
She settles back,
her rocker, the metalliferous lode
beyond the spray, guides
a breathing shore and shares
our veins in the lap.

LET HE WHO IS MORAL STEP FORWARD

Fiction by Steve Lester

I am the Earl of Leicester, 1st of the 8th creation, or 31st overall.[1] I am involved in courtly intrigue for the successor to Castlereagh, CEO of Great Britain.[2] I suspect that he suspects that I suspect his plan to establish a central bank. One day, after a session of parliament during which we yet again voted down a tax on private stills, I follow Castlereagh back to his office and surprise him while he is on the phone.

"Yes, I'd like to send this letter to the Pomeranian consulate in Dahomey by zeppelin. Am I too late for…" [3] He hangs up as soon as he notices me.

"Just dropping these off for you to sign in the morning," I say, waving some racing forms I picked up earlier at My Brother's Bar.[4] I see that Castlereagh's Burberry suspenders are undone. Then I notice the little hardbody sitting on his desk. "Am I interrupting something?"

"Leave them on my desk," Castlereagh says, turning his back to me. I recognize his mistress as Charlotte, one of Metternich's secretaries.[5] She is wearing a black dress by Coco Chanel and matching leather sneakers by Puma. "I guess you think I'm some sort of hypocrite."

"Who am I to judge?"

"Everyone judges. Who are you *not* to?"

"Does it matter?" I ask. Charlotte smiles with eye contact. I think she likes me.

"What do you mean?" Castlereagh asks back, still turned around.

"Well, perhaps I'm naïve, but I'm not sure personal ethics have anything to do with the art of statecraft."

"This is true." Castlereagh spins the globe next to his desk. The ocean is dust and each country is made out of a different precious stone. Prussia is electrum, Tanganyika is satinspar, and Siam is moolooite. "After me," Castlereagh continues, "no-one understands the affairs of the continent."

I take a stainless steel can opener by Brookstone in *SkyMall* out of my chamois skin jacket by Valentino and stab Castlereagh in the carotid artery. Blood covers the globe; I clean it off with a silk handkerchief by Prada. Then I place the can opener in Castlereagh's dominant hand.

"Hey," I say to Charlotte, "need a ride?"

***

We are at Eton,[6] an oft-trod field behind a plain white Victorian house. It is cold and cloudy outside. The entire House of Lords, including myself, are standing in a wide circle. The chamberlain is on the steps of the back porch. He is wearing an understated double-breasted beige suit by Brioni, a silk shirt and tie by Louis Vuitton, and Crocs. He claps once. This signals the beginning of the first test.

137

Everyone quiets, and there are twenty seconds of silence. It is broken by the chamberlain's speech, which is solemn and accurate:

"Let he who is moral step forward."

Several lords and I take one step forward, forming an inner circle. We are the pool of candidates from which Castlereagh's successor is to be chosen. John Wilmot, 2nd Earl of Rochester, stumbles forward later than everyone else.[7] He is wearing a blue pinstripe suit by P. Diddy, a shirt by Tommy Bahama, horn-rimmed glasses by Oliver Peoples, a silver nosepiece by The Sharper Image, and makeup by Rick Baker.[8] Everybody laughs except the chamberlain, who claps once and says:

"These men believe that they are moral. Very well. We shall find out if they are moral." The chamberlain looks around, and then continues. "The first test has come to pass. Now begins recess."

***

The chamberlain steps forward and claps twice. This signals the beginning of the second test. Everyone quiets, producing twenty seconds of silence. Then the chamberlain speaks, solemn, accurate:

"Let he who is moral step forward."

Two people step forward: me and John Wilmot. Many besides the chamberlain laugh, except people are also shocked and-or appalled. Lord Grey spits tea out his nose. Palmerston yells until Wellington boxes his ears. A lady from East Anglia and her daughter vomit. Gordon Brown wets himself. [9]

"These men believe that they are moral. Very well. We shall find out if they are moral." The chamberlain pauses, looks around, and continues. "The second test has come to pass. Now begins recess."

***

After the second test, Charlotte comes to my side. A reporter and her camera-fellow, a eunuch, approach.

"I'm here at the *playing fields of Eton* with the *Earl* of *Leicester*, Whig candidate for CEO of the Commonwealth." The reporter is a little blonde hardbody. She is wearing a plaid suit by Armani, a taupe shirt by Dolce and Gabbana, a bronzeberry frost silk scarf by Burberry, and gazelle skin loafers by Adidas. "People often refer to the *Earl of Rochester* having the will of the people," the hardbody continues, "as both a *good* and *bad* thing. Now, with the tragic loss of Lord Castlereagh and subsequent battle for succession, *John Wilmot* is your sole opposition. *Any thoughts on today's turn of events?*"

"I have the utmost respect for Rochester." I supplicate Castlereagh's ex-mistress' ass as I speak. "He is a great man, a great friend, and a worthy adversary. I can understand how some people might be opposed to his candidacy." I pause to watch Wilmot administer a philtre on the tongues of several admirers of both sexes using an eye-dropper by Williams-Sonoma. "But just because a man isn't moral doesn't mean he can't harness the morals of others to further the nation."

"Well, there you have it. Leicester, in a touch of class, harbors only *praise* for his opponent, the *controversial* Earl of Rochester. Let he who is moral, step forward! *Back to you,* Kent."

***

Several other lords are behind the garage with their wives, mistresses, and page-boys. The chamberlain is also here, but he just likes to watch. Charlotte is back here, too, smoking. She is wearing Seven-for-all-Mankind denim, a black v-neck tee by American Apparel, and red high heels by Manolo Blahnik. The ashes from her Parliament Light become dust mites as they return to the soil. We kiss. Opening my eyes, I notice two men approaching. They are brandishing unfinished cricket bats by Hammacher Schlemmer.

"I can explain, gentlemen."

"Let he who is moral step forward," the smaller one says, smacking the bat against his bare hand.

I take Charlotte by the hand, run across the field, and enter the house. We head up the concrete stairs. The walls are also concrete and barren. We stop every step to make out against the stairs and walls, which will hurt in the morning.

We enter a room on the third floor. There is a twin bed and a window. Charlotte jumps on and tugs at me.

"I know who you are," I say.

But you do not
answer. The sheets
are pond count,

infinitely many
Riemann surfaces
per square inch,

and you pull
me down
into you.

Endnotes

1 Leicester is pronounced "Lester." Cute, I know.

2 Robert Stewart, Viscount Castlereagh was born in Dublin on June 18, 1769 and committed suicide in Kent on August 12, 1822. He never served as the Prime Minister of the United Kingdom and, it is said, was the only statesman present at the Congress of Vienna (1814) that did not have a mistress. Though he was criticized in epigram by both Byron and Shelley, Castlereagh is now revered (notably by Henry Kissinger) for exercising a foreign policy far ahead of his time.

3 Adaptation of a Montgomery Burns quote in Simpsons episode 3F06, "Mother Simpson."

4 My Brother's Bar is a pub in downtown Denver.

5 Prince Klemens Wenzel von Metternich was born in Coblenz, Austria on May 15, 1773 and died in Vienna on June 11, 1859. Metternich was the Foreign Minister of Austria from 1809 until the revolutions of 1848, which were caused in part by his continuous suppression of liberal elements. During this time, he championed a "balance of power" diplomacy that both preserved Austria's precarious position and maintained relative peace in Europe following Napoleon. Metternich was also a patron to Beethoven, and, it is said, invented the female secretary, efforts without which the movie Secretary might still exist, but who knows?

6 The Duke of Wellington is famous for commemorating his victory over Napoleon at Waterloo by saying, "the battle of Waterloo was won on the playing fields of Eton." Except he never really said it. Good copy, though.

7 John Wilmot, 2nd Earl of Rochester, was born in Oxfordshire on April 1, 1647, and died (presumably from syphilis) there on July 26, 1680. The original libertine, Rochester was quite popular in the court of King Charles II, where he engaged in frivolities with a group of nobles and associated ne'er-do-wells known as The Merry Gang. Rochester was at turns a war hero, a patron of the arts, a louche and a profligate and, according to many admirers implicitly and Ezra Pound explicitly (in The ABC's of Reading), a key figure in the development of English-language poetry.

8 Rick Baker won an Academy Award in the category of Best Makeup Effects for his work on each of the following six films: An American Werewolf in London (1981), Harry and the Hendersons (1988), Ed Wood (1995), The Nutty Professor (1997), Men in Black (1998), Dr. Seuss' How

the Grinch Stole Christmas (2001).

9 Henry John Temple, 3rd Viscount Palmerston (1784 – 1865), served as Prime Minister on two non-consecutive occasions in the mid 19th century. Barney Gumble punches out Wade Boggs (and then, mistakenly, Moe) in Simpsons episode 8F13, "Homer at the Bat," culminating an argument over whether Palmerston or Pitt the Elder was the greatest British PM (Barney favors the former).

There have been six Earls Grey, a few of which were also Viscounts Howick, since the creation of the baronetcy. The second was Prime Minister and is known for the eponymous tea; the fourth has the Canadian Football League trophy named after him. At this trajectory, the sixth is estimated to be managing a Tesco.

Gordon Brown, however, is the current Prime Minister, and a total pussy.

COMMUNITY SUPPORTED, GRASSROOTS JOURNALISM.

WWW.MATTERDAILY.ORG

Blue Mirage

Fiction by Paul Miller

Mac drives down the baking road, forearm sticking to the dirty arm rest of the truck. Heat wavers in front of him in snaking ribbons, always out of reach on the horizon. He hits a rough stretch and the thump shakes his spine, makes him reach instinctively for another beer, if only he had any. Stopped drinking some time ago, save what's left of his kidneys, liver, what-not. Another bump lifts the welder in the back a few inches, slams it down hard. He hopes the rear tires have enough air. The welder will hold up. His back might not make it the 80 miles left to go.

Goddam blistering land, sky parched white, rain that never hits the ground, rabbitbrush and prickly pear like a carpet of nails. Stitch Mesa, passing by on the right, is a battleship of crumbling sandstone and secret recesses, his holy, sun-blasted playground when he was a kid, before the old man disappeared, before Mac started driving. Which doesn't mean much out here, kids driving when their noses reach above the steering wheel, independent by eight years old. Mac's old man, never could call him pa or dad, lived in adobe and dirt near a defile running through Stitch, with his wife and a brood of kids knocking into each other in the constant mess. Mac somewhere in the middle of the order. The family seized up often, could never figure out how to be ordinary. Place he grew up now claimed by mice and virus-infested scat.

At least his old man had given Mac the touch for working metal, must have been some rogue gene passing through. As a kid, Mac sat around watching sparks fly, peering through goggles too big for his head, iron joining in front of his eyes in beautiful, smooth beads. He sometimes wanted to ask the old man how he could weld two pieces of paper together, something he kept hearing from the old man's buddies, who dropped by to smoke and look sideways at Mac's sisters. But the old man never invited such conversation, retreating instead to the sweat lodge he'd

built, a pathetic attempt, Mac realized as an adult, to live like the Apaches, the old man's name for anybody who didn't look Anglo. Maybe, cleaning his pores in the lodge, the coot dreamed about riding bareback on some snorting mustang running like crazy on the high desert. He'd had enough dime-store artwork like that. Reality was, the old man could never get near a horse without risking a crushed skull.

Another jolt, another 60 miles to go. A small, warped wooden cross flashes past on the left. Memorial for his wife's pathetic brother. Wanted to be known as Chief, but everybody called him other names. Skinny son of a bitch, worthless beyond repair. At least he never married. Drove off the side of the road five years ago, cartwheeling a half-dozen times. Most of his body ended up a hundred feet from the twisted carcass of the car. Engine all by itself, leaking fluid into a wash. Engine mounting bracket may have failed, something Mac had warned him about. Wouldn't take much to fix, but of course the brother wouldn't have anything to do with it. Mac told his wife it was the mounting bracket, sure it was, just to soothe her. But her brother was drunk, distracted trying to roll a cigarette, swerve to hit a javelina, who knows. Now he's a monument to stupidity. The way she wept, turning her brother into a god. She cried, Mary did, for days. Five years ago, but Mac starting to think even then, he has to get out. Get rid of her. He can't breathe.

Mac snorts, thinking about the lie he'd tell her. "Mary, I'm gonna go look for the old man. I'll be back in a few years." She'd cry, but from laughing so hard. As if Mac gave a shit about daddy. An old story. "What's up with the job hunt," she'd ask. He hears her in his sleep sometimes. Mac would have to tell her, nothing. No job. People with a few hundred bucks, he was told by one greasy half-breed at a shop, can buy a welder from a catalog and do their own repairs. Machine may kill them, but there it is. Describing this, Mac would use up all his words for the rest of the week, trying to explain what it's like. Mary would be too quiet, look away for a long time. Maybe she's been thinking about leaving, too, as if life is nothing more than a dance out the door. Or maybe she'd explode.

He follows a long, shallow curve in the road, wonders how much gas is in the generator bolted to the bed of the truck near the welder. Out ahead, a single, dark comma floats in the heat, high above an arroyo. Too far away to tell what bird it is. Sits there, barely moving, then vanishes in the haze. He still loves her, he supposes. The way she whispers. Her insistent curiosity. Soft skin, elaborate braids, compact breasts, long waist. Easy to hate what's underneath, a squall like a badger. Her needs turning off and on like a light switch, taking his rough hands and moving them across her body, squeezing until he's light in the head, sick with desire. Next day, the switch is off, and he's a malignant stranger. Never know what to expect, walking into the house.

Something foreign ahead twitches him upright. Drive these roads too long and a piece of tailpipe stands out like a miracle. Mac squints, sees a dark shape, immobile. The shape becomes a car, then a pale blue Pontiac pulled over on the opposite side of the road. Mac slows, drives across the center line, stops with his front bumper ten feet from the Pontiac. Not your usual car for these parts. Expensive powder blue, dirt cooking into the finish. Swirls from a buffing pad stand out on the hood.

Mac takes a long look, finally sees something crumpled against the passenger's door. Late morning sun so bright, any shade becomes a black hole. Caution slows him to a crawl. Never know what you'll find. Once, he'd stopped to help a couple, said they were bird watchers. Not much birding available, he told them, then woke up twenty minutes later with a pint of his own blood soaking into the sand and his money gone. All fifty-six goddam dollars.

He opens the door of the truck, sidles toward the

car, skin prickling. His head feels like one single eyeball. On the passenger's side, he sees a swatch of long, straight hair through the closed window. He looks up and down the road, glances behind him. Nothing moving. Reaches out, gently raps the window. The figure inside bolts upright, sending Mac backpedaling, cursing. The face of a woman materializes in front of him, framed by the window. Or is it a woman? Hair cascading down, eyes blazing dark. Mac takes a quick look in the back seat, a jumble of blankets, clothes, plastic food containers, cardboard boxes. Hide a full-grown man back there, he'd never know.

The face in the window stares at him. Mac strains to hear something, but the only sound is his own thumping blood. He doesn't know what to do. The window slides down with an electric whir. He sees the keys on the steering column, has to be turned to accessory because the engine isn't running. Heat leaches out of the car, must be 200 stinking degrees inside.

It's a woman, eyes half closed as if pressing the window switch had sucked the life out of her. Strands of hair stick to her cheek. She tries making words, but her tongue seems swollen. She tries again. "Water?" she says.

She isn't from anywhere within five hundred miles. White shorts, damp around the edges, ride high and tight. Thighs look sunburned. Loose, long-sleeved blouse, something right out of a magazine, colors like a fizzing neon sign. Bright pink bra strap arcing over left shoulder.

"Sit tight," he says, glancing again into the back seat. Wouldn't be surprising to see a fucking rat traipsing around back there. He goes to the truck, hears the engine ticking like the heart of a robot, the only sound out here. No wind, unusual enough to mark on the calendar. He fetches a gallon jug of tepid water and a ceramic cup with a missing handle.

Mac hears a noise, jolts back. Only something shifting

in the truck. Why the hell is his heart racing like this? Forces himself to walk slowly back to the car, absorb everything, the way the Pontiac is angled off the road, glint of sun on the streaked windshield, Colorado license plate. A thousand miles north and a different galaxy from here.

She hasn't moved. He slops water into the cup, hands it through. A hand alive with rings wraps around the cup, tilts gingerly. Wrists so thin they'd break if you looked at them too hard.

He waits in the phosphorescent desert light, pulls his hat an inch lower on his forehead. The cup emerges from the car, and he pours more water. "Thanks," he hears. Then, "I feel sick."

Mac sets the jug down on pebbles coated with tar. "Don't know how else I can help," he says. Nothing moves, not even shadows. He wants to tell her help is a long way away. Being sick or being dead isn't all that important out here.

"Nothin you can do," she says. Her left hand, weighted with as much sparkle as the other, wavers near her ear, as if she's shooing a mosquito. "I'm waiting for my lover boy."

He looks hard at her. Sounded like Mary just then, poison cutting through you like a razor. Her face pleasantly thin and well angled, but her eyes wary torches. Canine teeth skewed a little forward. A few old, shallow scars, maybe from acne, cluster high on the outside ridge of her right cheek.

He waits.

She turns to face him, amused and annoyed he's still there. "Went off looking for psilocybin, heard it grew wild here, is that true?"

Mac sees paraphernalia on the console between the two seats, a drug emporium. No wonder her head's lolling like a broken spring. Never could do the stuff himself, when liquor was easier. His knees almost buckle, thinking about opening his throat to the forbidden, sweet oblivion.

"Maybe." He knew a few curanderos who mixed mushrooms with god knows what, ground bat bones, pulverized glass. Happy trails. "Easy enough to grow yourself."

"Oh, but he wants all natural," she sneers. Mac takes a step backward, scans the oven of landscape swallowing the horizon.

"So he's out there somewhere."

"That's right, kind stranger," changing mood like a kaleidoscope twisting on ball bearings. "He's huntin and gatherin, as he likes to say."

Mac feels queasy himself, picturing some squat white pigeon in sandals rooting around creosote bushes for mushrooms that don't exist. Twenty fucking minutes, and he's vulture snack.

"How long's he been gone?"

"Dunno. Few hours, I guess. What's your name, and where the hell are we?"

Of course the blue Pontiac doesn't start, making noises he isn't willing to deal with in the heat. She decides to hitch a ride with him to Shitpile, Nowhere, as she calls it, even though she's never seen it. The closest town, a scratch in the rock, but his other home when he isn't with Mary at their lean-to in the scrub. Mary has other names for their home, a generous three rooms and kitchen, but lean-to is the kindest she calls it.

Before the stranger lofts herself into the truck, missing a clean landing a couple of times, he makes her leave junk in the car. She wants to move wholesale, filling her arms with clothes, like the truck is a condo. Aspen, her name. Just like the goddam tree.

She's leaving boyfriend behind too easily. Too eager to accept Mac's suggestion that wandering off looking for the guy could kill both of them. But it's true: five minutes in a straight line and you vanish, melt into the maze. He knows enough trackers to know he's not one of them. She does leave a note for the goof, but shrugs when Mac asks about locking up. He leaves a gallon of water in the shade of the right front wheel.

He gears out onto the road, long bare legs filling the side of his vision, right breast a hillock pressing on insubstantial pink cotton. She's perked up a little. He keeps adding years to her age whenever he steals a glance. She doesn't so much as cut him a good look. What fun they'd have if she happened to knock open the glove compartment and discover his gun.

"No cell phone?" he asks.

"Battery's dead. Murkie carries it around with him all the time. Hooks it onto his pajamas whenever he wears them, too." Her half-laugh almost works.

"Murky," he says, thinking muddy water.

"What I call him, yeah. Mark."

The truck jolts. For the past hour, dealing with Aspen Tree, he'd forgotten about his back pain. She'd have, it occurs to him, enough pharmaceuticals to blast him to Mars. Gobble a handful and he could carry the truck to town. Or be too loopy to care.

Lupe, Mac's long-gone younger sister, springs fully formed into his head. Stranger beside him looks too much like her. Can't remember the last time he sat side-by-side with his sister on the mesa, kids knocking skinned knees together, tracking the waning crescent moon standing fat end down. They'd fill the crescent with berry syrup, honey, foaming milk.

"So," Aspen says, startling him. "What's our plan? Again?" She's starting to twitch like a bare wire shorting. Color not so good.

"Take a run into Shitpile, find some help for you and boyfriend. Can't guarantee much."

"You haven't guaranteed anything so far," she mumbles, and looks at him hard, like she's just now realizing what's going on. "What the fuck was in that water?" Her pupils are gone. Mac feels queasy in a new way. He pushes the truck faster, boiling dust behind in long funnel clouds.

Thirty minutes later, he rolls straight through town to Ma Bird at the clinic. Had to stop twice on the way to check if the stranger's heart had quit running. Jumps from the truck, squints through the front windows into the clinic. Ma's substantial form is coming toward him, slowly. She probably felt something was up hours ago. He learned early in his life to never ask how.

He pushes open the glass door, waits for Ma to nod at him. "Girl here's in trouble, Ma," he says. She nods again. He goes back to the truck, hoists Aspen into his arms. She's light, damp scraps of cloth on a doll. He maneuvers her into the clinic, lays her in a back room on an examining table covered with a paper sheet.

Ma Bird haunches up to the high table, opens the girl's right eyelid, inhales her breath. "Full of poison," she says. "Where'd you find her?"

"Bit west of Spar Wash. Boyfriend still out there somewhere, trying to kill himself." Ma's busy at a stainless steel counter pulling an intravenous rig and other gear from a cabinet. "I brought in some of the shit she was taking," he says. "Couldn't find any bottles with labels."

Ma takes the plastic bags, sets them carefully on the far edge of the counter. "Have to work now," she says. "You go tell Eddie."

Mac backs out of the room. Aspen is partly hidden by Ma's broad back. He sees the girl's feet, toenails painted bright blue, shin of her left leg scraped a little, like a kid who's played hard in a schoolyard. The sight catches him in a place he rarely pays attention to any more. He wants to stay, turn her hand over, study the wear marks and rings. She was so light in his arms, so loose and fractured.

His cousin Eddie signs off the radio. "Boys'll take a look soon as they can," he tells Mac. Eddie and the boys, the closest thing they have to real police, will find the blue Pontiac right away and maybe the boyfriend before dark. Heat doesn't kill you, chill of night will. At least in the daytime, you can see vultures circling. "They had something going on east side of town."

"I bet," Mac says. "Can't imagine anybody as busy as those two."

"All we got," Eddie says. Another old story. "Want to join the search?" Mac knows Eddie would rather go see the girl.

"Maybe later. Due over to Hardpan's to weld something." Well past noon, his stomach is saying.

The two regard the scattered history of Aspen on the table. Bent driver's license from Colorado. Thirty-four years old, heavier weight listed on the license than what he carried to Ma Bird. Address in Denver, could be some gated community or trailer park or barrio for all he knows. Couple of credit cards, both listing Ayasha as a first name. Chippewa, Eddie says. "Don't mean squat, tribe's never been west. Mommas saddling their kids with native names like it's some magic potion. Makes it easier on the rest of us, her using a tree for a nickname." A comb, melted tube of lip gunk, small bills and some change. Mac feels depression creeping in, settling. Nothing but loose junk to tell the girl's story. He sees blue toenail paint on the back of his closed eyelids.

Mac crickles his back upright, moves toward the door. His cousin never helps his mood, even on good days. Office a stifling wrack of ego. "What's your next move?"

"I may coast out there soon's I have lunch, have a look at the car," Eddie says. "Boys'll be there in a few hours, anyway. Clown like that, as easy to track as bulldozer treads. Maybe he lost his way back to the car."

Mac nods, steps into the heat. At least Eddie keeps the

office a comfortable 85 degrees. He drives slowly through town, past half-feral dogs, tumbleweeds stacked against leaning fences. He knows the houses, the canteens with cold beer, the old men leaning back in cracked wooden chairs waiting for the nuclear sun to go down. He looks at the place like Aspen might, and feels alien, spooked. All his life, Shitpile's been an oasis to him, a bump of buildings breaking the horizon, enough commerce to struggle along. A runt kid, he'd hitch to town on anything that moved and run around causing trouble, but enough of the right kind of adults there to cuff him into shape. Spent his adult life grinding dirt into his skin fixing ranch equipment, truck frames, I-beams with stress fractures. Sewed up a temporary guard rail once, where a van left the road on a curve coated with red mesa grit. For a long time, this place has been a tolerable fit. He doesn't have anything else.

He turns into an unnamed alley, passes a food store half the size of a boxcar, eases into a dirt parking lot. Hardpan needs something fixed at his printing business, Mac doesn't know what.

He parks next to a red pickup, shuts the engine off. Dogs bark way out. Before he opens the door, Hardpan comes out of the building, a big corrugated metal box.

"Hey, the sultan of steel," Hardpan brays. He's all chest and thick arms, paisley printer's bib dirty from years of ink and food. A steel-wool beard, once dark as his eyes, is frothed with white. A small chain runs in an arc from his belt buckle to a leather particulars nesting in the back pocket of his weary blue jeans. "Heard you coming a mile away and smelled you for two." Mac's hand disappears in his.

"Been destroying your equipment again, Hardguy?"

"With relish, I'm proud to say. Nah, table of my paper cutter broke, can't run long stock now." Hardpan's moving back toward the shop. "Some big idea of mine to move things around when they've sat just fine for a hundred years. Two fucking hundred. Tried lifting the cutter with a forklift, wanted to put rollers underneath, but snapped the corner right off." Inside, Mac is enveloped in an invisible cloud of ink, oil, cleaner, grease, solvent. Much as he's been around the stuff in other places, he forgets about it in seconds.

The shop is an open warehouse, printing equipment jammed against the sides and running down the middle. Skylights fogged with grime leach in a bit of light. An old platen press, a relic Hardpan retired years ago, is enthroned in the far back. Mac still hears the days when Hardpan's father talked about the press, the mechanics of feed board and grippers and ink disc creating so many impressions per hour. Now it's just Hardpan and a small Heidelberg press, a tiny bindery with a touchy folder and stitching machines. Mac's seen some of the publications Hardpan prints, admirable in an unusable way. He'd rather read blueprints and machine specs and manuals, all of them like a good mystery novel, figuring your way from one point to the next.

The cutter's a mess, but the break is at least clean. "Take a while to set up," Mac says. "Don't know if I can finish today. Can't guarantee the table'll be level either."

"Whatever you need, *muchacho*. I'll do what I can to get in your way. Whyn't you back your rig up and we'll get started." The men work until Hardpan hears Mac's stomach. He strides off, trailing talk, comes back 20 minutes later with lunch heaped in chilies and beans. "Honest down payment for your talent, *mi amigo*." Hardpan drinks beer, hands Mac opaque iced tea in a tall plastic glass. Hardpan chews, listens to Mac's truncated story about the girl. He studies Mac.

"Let's finish setting this up, then you can maybe weld the bad boy," Hardpan says. "We can fine-tune tomorrow. I have to find my grinder anyway, and that may take a while. Stay here tonight, hell, stay forever. You be my lackey, learn an honest trade for once." Mac grins through his fatigue, says okay. He hasn't talked so much in a year.

Late afternoon, Mac welds the piece back onto the cutter. "I'd call you a fucking genius, but you know that already, you weasel," Hardpan says. "Now go check your girlfriend, see if you can drag that Pontiac back with you. I need new struts."

Mac stops at Eddie's first, but nobody's home. At the clinic, Ma Bird takes him back to Aspen. She's in a tiny side room, looking like a corpse under a blanket. "Drained a lot of poison, but she needs to sleep out the rest," Ma says. "Take a while. Close call." Mac takes a long look at the girl's face, thin track of eyebrows, small doll nose. Color's better. Both arms under the blanket, tube running vertically. He resists uncovering an arm, weighted with its cargo of bangles.

"Thanks, Ma."

"Where's boyfriend? Eddie find out?"

"Don't know yet. I'm going out there now."

He stands until Ma Bird vanishes behind him, off to care for others, moving silent as a hunting cougar.

West of Spar Wash, Mac steps into a mess. Blue Pontiac missing all its fancy chrome wheels, doors and trunk open wide, litter surrounding the car. "Left the goddam engine for some reason," Eddie says. "Hell, they had a whole hour, plenty of time to take that, too, sons of bitch. Three of them, smooth-sole boots, probably at some chop shop right now. Like to just burn what's left, call it good." He may be pretending to be annoyed, Mac thinks, but the chrome wheels aren't likely in his truck. His hands are too clean. Twenty feet from the car, the boys' truck is pitched mostly off the road, rear bumper hanging into a lane.

"Boyfriend?" Mac asks.

"Still out there far as I know. Boys are taking long enough to find him. Goddam half-blind cub scout could do better. Can't wait to report them missing, too."

Mac scuffs out to a small rise in the desert a few hundred yards off the road, looks south into the labyrinth of scrub and cactus and canyon. Wind starting to pick up. Should call Mary, let her know. Rather be at the clinic, trying to fool himself into believing the stranger is his younger sister, back visiting from the dead, nothing but time on her hands. Too much alike, but Aspen thinner with a narrower face. About the right age. He doesn't want the boyfriend showing up, touching or looking at her. He's seen too much of this. She's better off without him, Mac feels in his bones. She needs a break.

Long shadows ease across the parched land, but the heat isn't lifting. Probably be a hundred degrees until well past midnight. He tells Eddie to keep him posted. "Oh, yah," Eddie bleats. "I'm up for election, so I need your vote."

At the clinic, Mac sits in a plastic chair beside Aspen Tree's bed. An intravenous bag reflects a bit of light from the hallway. He cringes at the creak in the chair, afraid of waking her.

He drifts off to the wide red mesa, far above the hovel where he grew up. The one time he saw his sister Lupe cry, she needed to get out. "I don't know, maybe it's the dust, the nothing, the waking up and knowing it'll all be the same as yesterday." Her bare heels excavating shallow ruts in the dirt, tears rolling down her cheeks, enough to fill a crescent moon and drown the sky. Something else there, but she never said. He didn't do enough for her, didn't do enough for the old man for that matter. Maybe it isn't too late for Mary.

Mac stays close to the sleeping woman for a few more hours, memorizes the tempo of her breathing.

His morning alarm is Hardpan crashing around in the print shop, cursing about a grinder. Mac's on a cot in an outbuilding, thinking about coffee. He sleeps again, accidentally. Hardpan wakes him with a sizzling pan of eggs, peppers, onions, potatoes, salsa, granulated sandstone. "Where's the ham?" Mac says. Hardpan swipes at his head, threatens to withhold the coffee.

The two work on the cutter, finally satisfied when the sun angles to late morning. "Mail you a few hundred tracts for payment, as if that'll cover the food I poured into you," Hardpan says. He settles with crumpled bills and a bag of chilies, sends Mac on his way.

Eddie is in. "Stupid shit walked right off rimrock a mile in," he says. "Had to go around a half-mile just to get to the pieces seventy feet down. Then haul him out. Do I look like I've been having fun?"

"What about the girl," Mac says.

"What about the girl? She can walk out of here at least."

"Does she know?

"About stupid shit? Yeah. She knows."

Ma Bird isn't in, but her lanky assistant is. Aspen is awake, sitting up. Her face looks like she's never learned how to smile.

"It's the kind stranger," she says.

"You remember."

"I remember a lot."

Mac waits.

"He wasn't my boyfriend, you know." Her eyes are welling.

"You were married."

She nods, runs a long finger across a cheek.

"We'll figure it out," he says. And he knows how. He'll take her back to her own home, stay until she says his name, just once, then head back to his lean-to in the scrub.

John Calderazzo

The Long Reach of Whale Songs

Late-summer Colorado drought.
I lie awake in bed
after midnight,
windows flung open.

For once, though,
no stars.
No moon
blueing the sagebrush foothills.

Rain soon,
I'm sure of it.
Rain for more reasons
than just these ripening clouds.

For the first time in months,
I hear boxcars
rumbling through town
more than eight miles away.

CONTRIBUTORS

Jessica Baron has just finished her MFA in poetry at Colorado State University in Fort Collins, Colorado. She has work out or forthcoming from *Matter, Wheelhouse, Parcel, Reconfigurations, and Mrs. Maybe.*

Matthew Britt is currently working on his second novel, *The Last Testament*, while staying at home with his three-year-old son, Farmer, and one-year-old daughter, Religion.

John Calderazzo teaches nonfiction writing at Colorado State University. He lives on a ridgetop with a windmill in beautiful Bellvue.

Chris Caruso received a BA from the University of Colorado at Boulder. His poetry has appeared in *Matter, Rio Grande Review, Lilliput,* and *Illiterate* as well as in the following anthologies: *The Hay(na)ku Anthology, Vol 2* and *Zeus Seduces the Wicked Stepmother in the Saloon of the Gingerbread House: Myth, Fairy Tale and Legend for the 21st Century.*

Kurt Caswell spent the last semester teaching in Seville, Spain, loving every minute of it. His most recent book, *An Inside Passage,* (published by University of Nebraska Press) won the River Teeth Literary Nonfiction Prize and contains two essays published in *Matter* (An Inside Passage, and Banaue Tercet).

Paul DeHaven plays music with Paper Bird and writes things. Sometimes he sits still in the woods and weaves. Other times he travels/tours on a school bus named Schoolie, the Great White Dinosaur. Colorado is home, because of the way the clouds wrestle the sun and the way the sun usually wins.

Dawn Dennison lives in Nederland, Colorado with her husband, Tom, some dogs and a horse. She works for a non-profit organization and is a volunteer firefighter. Her fiction has been nominated for a Pushcart Prize. She makes very flaky piecrusts.

Mark DeRespinis has been wild caught in a variety of ways, held for a moment to a shadow impression of words on the page, or images fallen into a definite pattern, or glimpsed in bizarre bodily contortions in-between darkness and light.

Sue Ring deRosset speaks the special language now only known to sacred waterfowl, Palamino horses, and cats of all varieties. With editing skills unparalleled and eyes set to the moon, she thrives surrounded in words, Williams, and animals.

Brian Dickson has lived mostly in the southwest working various jobs and now finds himself living in Colorado teaching at various grade levels. He plans on living in the West before it fills up and will continue riding his bike. Some publications include *Santa Clara Review, Switchback, Goodfoot, The Blue Mesa Review,* and others.

Megan Guidarelli is a senior Theatre and Creative Writing double major at CSU.

Elliott Johnston writes about music and other things. He contributes regularly to *5280 Magazine, Boulder Weekly, Kansas City Pitch* and *Dallas Observer.* He has also written for *Arthur Magazine* and spent several formative years as a staffer for the defunct Fort Collins alt-weeklies *Rocky Mountain Bullhorn* and *Rocky Mountain Chronicle.*

Ryan Kerr teaches English and Drama at a small high school in the northwestern suburbs of Milwaukee, WI. Apart from teaching courses in AP Language and Creative Writing, he also directs the school's musical and stage productions.

Just Kibbe can neutralize, pluck, and eviscerate a chicken in less than five minutes. An ex-Marine, he was awarded the "Pizza Box" for his lack of prowess on the rifle range. Just Kibbe, with two co-captains – Nate Mohatt & M. Thomas Russell – built his own ship, the Pirate Pig Press, which he's learned is more difficult to steer than a bull through a heifer pen.

Julie Larson lives in New York and wants to get back to Mongolia.

M. K. Leonard lives and writes in Colorado, has two sons, one daughter, and one son-in-law. She has never gone up in a hot air balloon and is visited now and then by a Sheltie spirit. She thinks people owe the Third Rock and not the other way 'round.

Stephen Charles Lester previously appeared in *Matter 8: Land.* His work has also recently been featured in *Iconoclast, failbetter, DIAGRAM,* and *Juked*. He is a senior business analyst at a software company in Denver.

Charles Malone likes: lifting heavy objects, biking, Susan, and riding on zip-lines. Charles Malone does not like: doing dishes.

Paul Miller, editor of *Colorado State Magazine* at CSU, has published creative nonfiction in books and literary magazines including *Pulse of the River, The Sand Papers, Wild Things, Orion,* and a forthcoming anthology by University of Oklahoma Press (2009).

David Mitchell likes to take photographs and ride his bicycle east.

Blair Oliver's story collection, *Last Call*, was published in 2007. His crime novel, *The Long Slide*, will be available this fall from Ghost Road Press.

Esme Patterson has several irons in the fire. There's no saying which ones are hot, however.

Leslie Patterson's stories and essays have appeared in *Fourth Genre, Bellevue Literary Review, Ballyhoo Stories, Matter,* the 2007 Fish Publishing Prize Anthology, and *Big Land, Big Sky, Big Hair: Best of the Texas Poetry Calendar's First Decade.* She is currently working on a historical novel and lives in Fort Collins, Colorado.

Jessy Randall's collection of poems, *A Day in Boyland* (Ghost Road Press, 2007) was a finalist for the Colorado Book Award. She has a young adult novel, *The Wandora Unit*, forthcoming in 2009.

Susan Hazel Rich works as graphic artist and spends many creative hours designing and sewing one-of-a-kind handmade clothing. She enjoys throwing lavish dinner parties in her town home and haggling with bike thieves at her second residence.

Jared Schickling is in the MFA program at CSU. His work has appeared in some places, and he has two poetry books with Blazevox, *Aurora* (2007) and *Submissions* (2008). He also has an essay in the next issue of *Jacket*.

Michael G. Smith has been published in *Bellowing Ark, Edgz, Kaleidoscope, Matter, Nimrod, Sulphur River Literary Review* and other journals. Poetry is forthcoming in the *Santa Fe Literary Review*. He is spending this summer in Bozeman, MT, growing crystals, hiking and biking.

Dona Stein, a former Wallace Stegner Fellow in Poetry at Stanford University, recently received a Colorado Humanities Grant for an anthology of guests on The Poetry Show at KRFC 88.9fm from among the last six and half years she has produced and hosted the program.

Susan Tepper is a poet writing in Fort Collins and is currently attending the Colorado State University MFA program in poetry. Her work has recently appeared in *CAB/NET* journal.

J Michael Wahlgren is the author of two chapbooks: *Chariots of Flame* (2007) & *Pre-elixir* (2008) both on Maverick Duck Press & the full-length poetry collection *Silent Actor* (BeWrite, 2008). He resides in Boston, Ma where he edits & web designs Eight Octaves.

Kathleen Willard is an ardent student of poetry and has two advanced degrees: MA in Literature form Middlebury College and an MFA in Creative Writing from Colorado State University. She received a Fulright-Hays Fellowship to travel and study in India and a national Endowment for the Humanities grant to study writers of the New England Renaissance in Massachusetts.

Joshua Zaffos is a freelance journalist in Fort Collins who has worked as a staff writer and editor for several independent weeklies in northern Colorado, and holds a master's degree from the Yale School of Forestry and Environmental Studies. He has written for *High Country News, Orion, Grist, Fly Fisherman, 5280.com*, and a number of other print and online publications.

Felicia Zamora thrives from the curious world. Every night, she opens the front door at dusk to smell the air. During the day, she's an undergraduate advisor and creative writing student. Other published works may be found in *Academic Advising Today, Poetrybay, Ruminate, Matter, The Great Ecstatic Reporter,* and *Walt's Corner.*

Local Food

Community Focused
Farmer Friendly

Member Owned

the FOOD CO-OPERATIVE

your naturally local grocery market • FORT COLLINS, COLORADO | SINCE 1972

Front Range Review, the literary magazine
published by the creative writing program at
Front Range Community College, seeks quality
short fiction, poetry, and creative nonfiction for
its annual issue. Our reading period is August
15th — December 1 each year.

Send your best work to:

Blair Oliver, Faculty Advisor
Front Range Review, FRCC,
4616 S. Shields, Fort COllins, CO 80526

thought provoking

vital

inspire

diverse discussion

expression

COLLABORATE

intellectual human

community

creative

catalyst

ENGAGE

ENVIRONMENT

learning

everyone

EXPERIENCE

beet
STREET

FORT COLLINS, COLORADO

art.
culture.
science.
everyone.

WWW.BEETSTREET.ORG

SUSAN HAZEL RICH   PRINT & WEB DESIGNER   ONE OF A KIND HANDMADE CLOTHING
please save forever [or recycle]   client list & portfolio at www.susanhazelrich.com   shop & browse clothing at www.susanhazelrich.etsy.com

SEE
Fort Collins
By Bicycle

FCBIKE
Library

WWW.FCBIKELIBRARY.ORG

The CENTER for JUSTICE PEACE and ENVIRONMENT

Our mission is to create community based on furthering economic, social, and environmental justice, sustainability, human rights, and peace for all by building coalitions, developing strategies and actions, and supporting existing progressive organizations.

www.cjpe.org 970.419.8944

Print YourJob.com

Your Local Online Print Alternative

www.printyourjob.com

(970) 672-4933

Powered by pixelsandpress.com pixels&press

Economical Printing
Green Delivery
Free Online Design Tool
Recycled Options
Quick Digital Printing

Where you **go** o go **green...**

F YOU OWN A 3USINESS:

each conscious consumers
cally or nationally by listing in the
ost comprehensive green business
atabase with a local focus.

et 5x the exposure by also being
ted on our partner sites: National
eographic, Ecobroker, Newscorp
d 9News. Reap the benefits of
ese extensive partnerships and
filiate programs.

btain green business certification
rough the multi-level GenGreen
ertification program.

omote your business through
e events calendar, job board and
stainable Savings section.

IF YOU'RE A PERSON:

**Find over 45,000 green businesses
and non-profit organizations**
across the U.S. and in 20 categories,
including green retailers, restaurants,
arts and entertainment, travel,
parks and recreation, recycling,
transportation and more.

Find local and national **green events,
green collar jobs** and **volunteer
opportunities**.

Get discounts from your favorite
green businesses in the Sustainable
Savings section.

Get daily green tips and **learn how
easy it can be** to live an eco-
conscious lifestyle.

GenGreen®*life*

Find the green in everything

www.gengreenlife.com

Proudly owned and operated in Fort Collins, Colorado.

MATTER 13 EDWARD ABBEY

Now seeking submissons of fiction, nonfiction, poetry, art, photography, and ephemera for our 13th issue exploring the writer Edward Abbey. Submissions must be postmarked by December 1st, 2009. For more information, please visit www.wolverinefarmpublishing.org.